50 Tunisian STITCHES™

DARLA J. FANTON

Contents

Tunisian Basic Information

The origins of Tunisian crochet are unknown. Patterns for projects using the technique began appearing in the mid-19th century in publications such as *Weldon's Practical Needlework*. Often referred to as tricot stitch in those early publications, it is also unknown where the term "Tunisian crochet" originated.

Somewhat of a cross between knitting and crochet, Tunisian crochet is worked on a long hook with a knob on one end. Some people believe it represents a missing link between knitting and crochet. There are knit and purl stitches in Tunisian crochet that lend some credibility to that theory.

HOOKS

A few years ago, Tunisian hooks were difficult to find in any material other than aluminum unless they were custom made by a woodworker. Lengths were limited to around 14 inches, and sizes ranged from around 4mm to 6.5mm.

With the recent resurgence of interest in Tunisian crochet has come a variety of new hooks from many different companies. Straight hooks are now available in a variety of lengths, materials and sizes. Hooks with a cable and button end in various sizes are particularly helpful when working a large project as they allow the weight of the project to rest in your lap instead of on the hook, thus allowing you to avoid shoulder and arm strain. Most recently, interchangeable hook sets have hit the marketplace. These allow you to select the cord length most appropriate for the number of stitches you are working with.

GETTING STARTED

It is possible to create either a firm, dense fabric or a light and lacy fabric with Tunisian crochet. The finished fabric is influenced by the diameter of the hook, the weight of the yarn and the Tunisian stitch pattern.

For instance, Tunisian simple stitch creates a firm, thick fabric if worked with the same size hook you would ordinarily use for standard crochet. To produce a softer fabric with more drape, simply use a Tunisian hook several sizes larger or use a lighter weight yarn.

Tunisian crochet is usually worked with the same side facing you at all times. This is usually considered the right side, although in some stitch patterns both sides are equally attractive.

Most people find holding the Tunisian hook with their hand above the hook, resting lightly over the stitches, with their index finger extended the most comfortable position and provides the best control.

Each row consists of 2 actions: the forward motion where you pick up the loops (stitches) and hold them on the hook, followed by the return motion where you work the loops off the hook until only one loop remains. The loop that remains on the hook after completing the return motion counts as the first stitch of the next row. If you are right-handed, you will be working the pick-up or forward pass of the row from right to left and the return portion from left to right. A row is considered completed when you are back to the right-hand edge of the work with one loop left on the hook.

The pick-up portion of a row results in vertical bars which always come in pairs—one strand to the front of the work and one strand to the back. The return pass of the row creates a line of horizontal "chains" that runs between the vertical bars. (see Photo A)

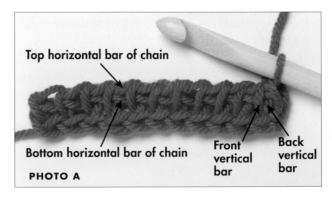

Top horizontal bar of chain

Bottom horizontal bar of chain

Front vertical bar

Back vertical bar

PHOTO A

An endless variety of stitches can be created based on where you pick up stitches for the next row as well as how many stitches you work off at a time during the return pass.

FOUNDATION ROW

The first row is often referred to as the foundation row and is usually, although not always, worked in the same manner: Using either the Tunisian hook or a standard length hook, chain the desired number of stitches. If using a standard hook, transfer the final loop on the hook to the Tunisian hook. Gently roll the chain toward you to expose the bumps on the back of the chain, insert the hook under the second bump from the hook, bring the yarn over the hook from back to front and draw it through the bump, forming a loop on the hook. Continue in the same manner, picking up a stitch in each bump on the chain. At the end, you should have the same number of stitches on the hook as were in the starting chain. (see Photo B)

PHOTO B

To work the stitches off the hook: Bring the yarn over the hook from back to front and draw through the first lp (see Photo C), *yo, draw through the next 2 lps (see Photo D), rep from * until 1 lp rem on the hook. This is the method most often, although not always, used to work the stitches off the hook and is sometimes referred to as a "standard return."

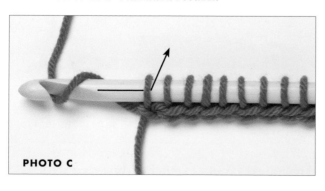

PHOTO C

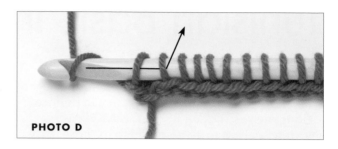

PHOTO D

Because the loop remaining on your hook is the first stitch of the next row, unless instructed otherwise, you will skip the first vertical bar (the one directly below the loop on your hook) as you begin to pick up stitches for the next row. (see Photo E)

Skip first vertical bar

PHOTO E

No matter what stitch you work in subsequent rows, the final stitch of each row requires special attention. Because the first stitch of the row (the one on your hook after the return) never varies, you want to match this stitch at the end of the row. Insert the hook under both the front and back vertical bars, yarn over and draw through. This creates a nice firm edge. This is basically the same as the Tunisian knit stitch, but when worked as the last stitch of the row, it is usually written as "Tunisian simple stitch under both strands." (see Photo F)

PHOTO F

REFINING YOUR WORK

Once you understand how to create stitches, you can work on the little things that can have a big impact on the appearance of your work.

Working Tension: You want to work with a smooth, even tension on both the pick up and return portions of the row. When picking up stitches, be sure to bring the loop up to the full height of the row. In other words, the hook should rest above the previous row, not on top of it.

Practice the return portion until the stitches are even. If you work the return too tightly, you will restrict the width of your piece and the vertical bars may look crowded. Work the return too loosely and you will see untidy little loops of excess yarn appearing.

I find the overall appearance to be most appealing when all four edges have an even chain-link appearance.

Bottom Edge: Picking up in the bump on the wrong side achieves the chain-link appearance. If the foundation row is too tight, your piece will draw in at the bottom. One way to correct this is to crochet the beginning chain with a hook one size larger and then switch to the desired size as you pick up stitches.

Right Edge: Since the loop at the beginning of the row is always on the hook, this edge can become too loose. There are a couple of options to correct this problem. The first method is during the forward pass when you have two loops on the hook, stop and pull up on the second loop, which causes the end stitch to tighten, and then readjust the working yarn to tighten the second stitch and continue on. For the second method, at the end of the return portion when only one loop remains on the hook, remove that loop and place it on a locking stitch marker. Continue to pick up loops as indicated in the pattern. (see Photo G) On the return portion of the row, remember to replace the marked stitch on the hook and work it off in the normal fashion. (see Photo H)

PHOTO G

Remove this loop from hook. Place loop that is on stitch marker onto hook. Replace this loop back on hook. Yarn over and draw through final 2 lps on hook.

PHOTO H

Left Edge: Success on this edge depends on ensuring that you are inserting the hook under both loops of the final stitch. From my years of teaching, I know this can be hard to see for beginners because the first horizontal stitch from the previous return often lies over and mimics the vertical edge stitch. I developed the following method to help students become accustomed to seeing where to insert the hook for the final stitch of the next row. After picking up all stitches in the row, place a locking stitch marker around the final stitch on the hook and the working yarn. (see Photo I) Work the standard return as normal.

The location to insert the hook for the final stitch of the next row is now clearly marked. (see Photo J)

PHOTO I

PHOTO J

Top Edge: After the return portion of the final row, the work will look a bit open and unfinished. The final step is referred to as the bind-off. It is most often worked using a slip stitch but can be worked using single crochet or other stitches as instructed.

CURL & BIAS

Some Tunisian stitches will cause your work to curl. This is just their nature. Tunisian simple and knit stitches do have this tendency. But don't despair—there are ways to deal with the curl. Using a larger hook helps relax the fabric. You can start and end your project with Tunisian stitches that do not have a tendency to curl, such as purl stitch or reverse stitch. Working a border of standard crochet stitches will counterbalance the curl. Blocking will help reduce the curl. I have also found that yarns with a high nylon content do not curl as readily.

Or you may decide to use the curl to your advantage as a design feature as I have done in the roll-brim hat on page 47.

Some stitches have a tendency to bias, slanting to either the right or the left. If only one edge is developing a diagonal slant, you will want to check that you are not either losing or adding a stitch at the beginning or end of the rows. If both edges are slanting equally, it may just be a characteristic of that particular pattern stitch. This tendency is not always easy to predict. In general, if a small swatch is biasing, the bias will be more obvious when worked in a full-scale project. Sometimes it can be corrected by blocking. At other times, such as in a scarf or shawl, it can become a design feature. Or you may decide to just live with it; a throw in the shape of a parallelogram can be just as warm and cozy as a rectangle.

CHANGING COLORS

You will notice a much different look depending upon where additional colors are introduced in Tunisian crochet. Changing color at the beginning of the return portion of a row (in other words, the left edge) results in a woven or tweed effect. In order to create a stable left edge, the color being dropped must be "locked in." When picking up a previously dropped color, always pick it up from underneath the current color. (see Photos K, L and M)

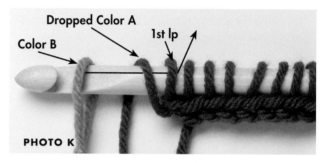

PHOTO K

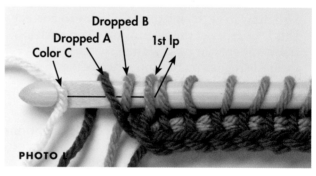

PHOTO L

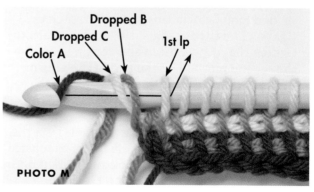

PHOTO M

Changing color at the beginning of the forward pass of a row (in other words, the right edge) results in solid stripes. Because first stitch of a row actually happens with the last action of the return pass, that is where you will change colors. Carry the unused color(s) neatly along the right edge in order to avoid long floats. When picking up a previously dropped color, always pick it up from underneath the current color. (see Photos N, O, P and Q)

Before working any of the patterns using more than one color, we urge you to work through the Tricolor Tweed and Tricolor Stripe patterns in order to gain valuable knowledge on how to carry the unused colors neatly along the side. ∎

Dropped A

1st vertical bar will be skipped

PHOTO O

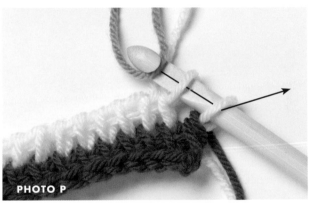

PHOTO P

PHOTO N

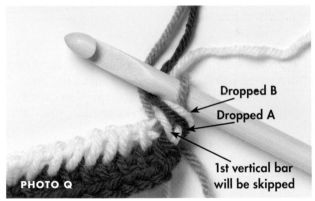

Dropped B

Dropped A

1st vertical bar will be skipped

PHOTO Q

Tunisian Simple Stitch (tss)

Multiple of any number

PATTERN NOTE

This is the most basic Tunisian stitch. It forms an even grid and has often been used as the base for intricate cross-stitch patterns. Also called afghan stitch, this stitch has a tendency to curl.

INSTRUCTIONS

Row 1: Ch desired number, working in **back bump** (see illustration) of chs, pick up a lp in 2nd ch from hook and in each rem ch across, leaving all lps on hook.

Back Bar of Chain

Row 1 return: Yo, draw through 1 lp on hook, *yo, draw through 2 lps on hook, rep from * until 1 lp rem on hook.

Row 2: *Insert hook from right to left under next vertical bar, yo and draw through, keeping lp

on hook, rep from * across, picking up under both strands of final st.

Row 2 return: Rep row 1 return.

Rep row 2 for desired length. Bind off. ∎

Tunisian Knit Stitch (tks)

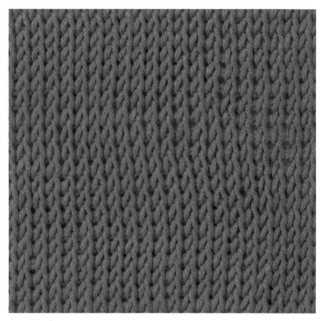

Multiple of any number

PATTERN NOTES

This stitch looks like stockinette stitch in knitting; however, it is denser than stockinette. Like stockinette stitch, it has a tendency to curl.

INSTRUCTIONS

Row 1: Ch desired number, working in **back bump** (see illustration) of chs, pick up lp in 2nd ch from hook and in each rem ch across, leaving all lps on hook.

Back Bar of Chain

Row 1 return: Yo, draw through 1 lp on hook, *yo, draw through 2 lps on hook, rep from * until 1 lp rem on hook.

Row 2: *Insert hook from front to back between strands of next vertical bar, yo and draw through, keeping lp on hook, rep from * across, picking up under both strands of last st.

Row 2 return: Rep row 1 return.

Rep row 2 for desired length. Bind off in sl st as if to tks. ■

Tunisian Purl Stitch (tps)

Multiple of any number

PATTERN NOTES

This stitch features a horizontal bar on the right side of the work, reminiscent of the purl bump in knitting. This stitch does not curl and is often used as a border stitch to control the tendency of other stitches to curl. It is also used in combination with other stitches to create contrasting textures. Unlike most Tunisian stitches in which the yarn remains to the back of the work, for purl, the yarn must come to the front first. The easiest way to do this is to flick it to the front with your hook. When you move the yarn across the stitch and to the back, a horizontal bar is created at the base of the vertical bar. It is helpful to anchor this bar with your thumb as you complete the stitch.

This stitch can form a gap at the left edge if a standard return is worked. For this reason I begin the return with yarn over, draw through 2 loops. This results in the last 2 vertical bars at the left edge being connected at the top. Technically, this is a decrease so it is important to remember to pick up a loop in each of the stitches unless you intend to decrease.

INSTRUCTIONS

Row 1: Ch desired number, working in **back bump** (*see illustration*) of chs, pick up a lp in 2nd ch from hook and in each rem ch across, leaving all lps on hook.

Back Bar of Chain

Row 1 return: *Yo, draw through 2 lps on hook, rep from * until 1 lp rem on hook.

Row 2: *With yarn to front, insert hook under next vertical bar as if to work **tss** (*see page 8*), bring yarn across front of vertical bar and to back, yo and draw through, keeping lp on hook, rep from * across, picking up under both strands of last st with yarn staying to back.

Row 2 return: Rep row 1 return.

Rep row 2 for desired length. Bind off. ■

Tunisian Reverse Stitch (trs)

Multiple of any number

PATTERN NOTES

This stitch looks similar to **Tunisian purl stitch** (*see page 9*), but the mechanics of working it are different. If you prefer working this stitch, it can often be successfully substituted for purl in a pattern. It is another stitch that can be used to counterbalance the curl.

Like Tunisian purl stitch, this stitch can form a gap at the left edge if a standard return is used.

INSTRUCTIONS

Row 1: Ch desired number, working in **back bump** (*see illustration*) of chs, pick up a lp in 2nd ch from hook and in each rem ch across, leaving all lps on hook.

Back Bar of Chain

Row 1 return: *Yo, draw through 2 lps on hook, rep from * until 1 lp rem on hook.

Row 2: *Insert hook under back strand of next vertical bar, yo and draw through, keeping lp on hook, rep from * across, picking up under both strands of last st.

Row 2 return: Rep row 1 return.

Rep row 2 for desired length. Bind off. ∎

Extended Tunisian Simple Stitch (extss)

Multiple of any number

PATTERN NOTES

The extra height of this stitch seems to counter-balance the curl; it also tends to have a "softer" hand than Tunisian simple stitch.

You can also work this stitch by inserting the hook as if to work **Tunisian knit stitch** (*see page 8*) followed by a chain 1. This would be an extended Tunisian knit stitch (extks).

INSTRUCTIONS

Row 1: Ch desired number, working in **back bump** (*see illustration*) of chs, pick up lp in 2nd ch from hook and in each rem ch across, leaving all lps on hook.

Back Bar of Chain

Row 1 return: Yo, draw through 1 lp on hook, *yo, draw through 2 lps on hook, rep from * until 1 lp rem on hook.

Row 2: Ch 1, *insert hook from right to left under next vertical bar, yo and draw through, ch 1, keeping lp on hook, rep from * across, picking up under both strands of last st, ch 1.

Row 2 return: Rep row 1 return.

Rep row 2 for desired length. Bind off. ■

Tunisian Double Stitch (tds)

Multiple of any number

PATTERN NOTE

Essentially, this is like working a double crochet without pulling through the last 2 loops of the stitch.

INSTRUCTIONS

Row 1: Ch desired number, working in **back bump** (*see illustration*) of chs, yo, pick up lp in 3rd ch from hook, yo, draw through 2 lps on hook, *yo, pick up lp in next bump, yo, draw through 2 lps, rep from * across, leaving all lps on hook.

Back Bar of Chain

Row 1 return: Yo, draw through 1 lp on hook, *yo, draw through 2 lps on hook, rep from * until 1 lp rem on hook.

Row 2: Ch 1, *yo, pick up lp under next vertical bar, yo and draw through 2 lps, keeping lp on hook; rep from * across until 1 st rem, yo, pick up under both strands of last st, yo, draw through 2 lps.

Row 2 return: Rep row 1 return.

Rep row 2 for desired length. Bind off. ■

Tunisian Full Stitch (tfs)

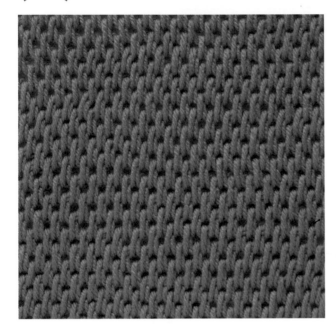

Multiple of any number

PATTERN NOTES
These stitches are picked up between vertical bars, working under the horizontal connecting stitches. In order to keep work from biasing, you must alternate placement of first stitch of row.

INSTRUCTIONS
Row 1: Ch desired number, working in **back bump** *(see illustration)* of chs, pick up a lp in 2nd ch from hook and in each rem ch across, leaving all lps on hook.

Back Bar of Chain

Row 1 return: Yo, draw through 1 lp on hook, *yo, draw through 2 lps on hook, rep from * until 1 lp rem on hook.

Row 2: Pick up lp in sp before next st, *pick up lp in next sp, rep from * across.

Row 2 return: Rep row 1 return.

Row 3: Sk first sp, *pick up lp in next sp, rep from *, ending **tss** *(see page 8)* under both strands of last st.

Row 3 return: Rep row 1 return.

Rep rows 2 and 3 for desired length. Bind off in pattern. ■

Tunisian Twisted Stitch (ttws)

Multiple of any number

INSTRUCTIONS
Row 1: Ch desired number, working in **back bump** *(see illustration)* of chs, pick up a lp in 2nd ch from hook and in each rem ch across, leaving all lps on hook.

Back Bar of Chain

Row 1 return: Yo, draw through 1 lp on hook, *yo, draw through 2 lps on hook, rep from * until 1 lp rem on hook.

Row 2: *Using notched area of hook, snag front vertical bar of next st from left to right, twist hook down and around, forming a twist in bar, yo and pull up lp, rep from * across until 1 st rem, **tss** *(see page 8)* under both strands of last st.

Row 2 return: Rep row 1 return.

Rep row 2 for desired length. Bind off. ∎

Drop Stitch

Multiple of any number

INSTRUCTIONS

Row 1: Ch desired number, working in **back bump** *(see illustration)* of chs, pick up a lp in 2nd ch from hook and in each rem ch across, leaving all lps on hook.

Back Bar of Chain

Row 1 return: Yo, draw through 1 lp on hook, *yo, draw through 2 lps on hook, rep from * until 1 lp rem on hook.

Row 2: Tks *(see page 8)* in each st across, until 1 st rem, tss under both strands of last st.

Row 2 return: Rep row 1 return.

Row 3: Ch 1, *yo, tks in next st, rep from * across until 1 st rem, yo, **tss** *(see page 8)* under both strands of last st. *(number of sts on hook should be twice number of beg chs minus 1)*

Row 3 return: Ch 2, *carefully remove lp from left end of hook, allow yo to drop off left end of hook, place lp back on hook, yo, draw through 2 lps on hook, rep from * across until 1 lp rem on hook.

Row 4: Rep row 2, working last tss in 2nd ch of beg 2 chs of previous row return.

Row 5: Rep row 2.

Rep rows 2–5 for desired length. Bind off in sc as if to tks.

Block to even out elongated dropped sts. ∎

Offset Star Stitch

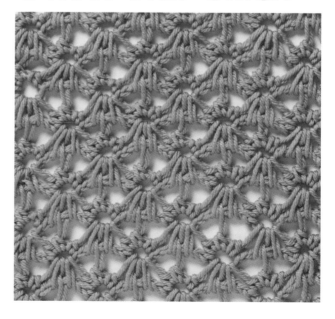

Multiple of 6 + 5

PATTERN NOTE

When picking up loop in spaces, insert hook under horizontal connecting stitches as in **Tunisian full stitch** *(see page 12)*.

INSTRUCTIONS

Row 1: Ch desired number, working in **back bump** (see illustration) of chs, pick up a lp in 2nd ch from hook and in each rem ch across, leaving all lps on hook.

Back Bar of Chain

Row 1 return: Yo, draw through 1 lp on hook, *yo, draw through 2 lps on hook, rep from * until 1 lp rem on hook.

Row 2: Ch 1, **tds** (see page 11) in each of next 2 sts, *3 tss, 3 tds, rep from * across until 2 sts rem, **tss** (see page 8), tss under both strands of last st.

Row 2 return: Ch 1, yo, draw through 3 lps on hook, *ch 2, yo, draw through 2 lps on hook, ch 2, yo, draw through 6 lps on hook, rep from * across until 3 lps rem, ch 2, [yo, draw through 2 lps on hook] twice.

Row 3: Tss, *pick up lp in sp before next cluster, 3 tds in top of next cluster, pick up lp in sp after cluster, tss, rep from * across until 1 partial cluster rem, pick up lp in sp before last partial cluster, 2 tds in top of last partial cluster.

Row 3 return: Yo, draw through 1 lp on hook, *ch 2, yo, draw through 6 lps on hook, ch 2, yo, draw through 2 lps on hook, rep from * across until 5 lps rem, ch 2, yo, draw through 4 lps on hook, yo, draw through 2 lps on hook.

Row 4: Ch 1, 2 tds in top of partial cluster, pick up lp in sp after partial cluster, *tss, pick up lp in sp before next cluster, 3 tds in top of next cluster, pick up lp in sp after cluster, rep from * across until 1 st rem, tss under both strands of last st.

Row 4 return: Rep row 2 return.

Rep rows 3 and 4 for desired length. Work last return as for row 1 return. Bind off in sl st. ■

Star Stitch

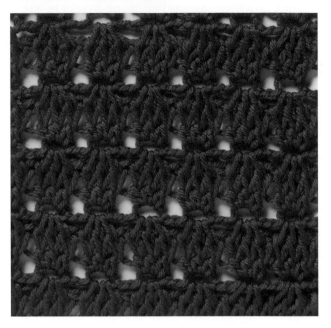

Multiple of 3 + 2

INSTRUCTIONS

Row 1: Ch desired number, working in **back bump** (see illustration) of chs, pick up a lp in 2nd ch from hook and in each rem ch across, leaving all lps on hook.

Back Bar of Chain

Row 1 return: Yo, draw through 1 lp on hook, ch 1, *yo, draw through 4 lps on hook, ch 1, rep from * across to last 2 lps, yo draw through last 2 lps.

Row 2: Ch 1, 3 **tds** (see page 11) in top of each cluster across until 1 st rem, **extss** (see page 10) under both strands of last st.

Row 2 return: Yo, draw through 1 lp on hook, *yo, draw through 2 lps on hook, rep from * across until 1 lp rem on hook.

Row 3: Tks (see page 8) in each st across until 1 st rem, **tss** (see page 8) under both strands of last st.

Row 3 return: Rep row 1 return.

Rep rows 2 and 3 for desired length. Bind off in sl st as if to trs. ∎

Braided Stitch

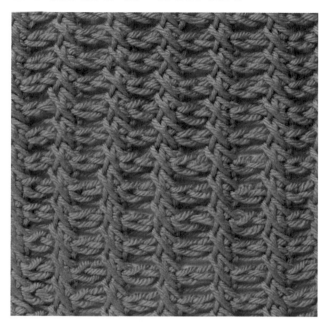

Multiple of 3 + 2

INSTRUCTIONS

Row 1: Ch desired number, working in **back bump** *(see illustration)* of chs, pick up a lp in 2nd ch from hook and in each rem ch across, leaving all lps on hook.

Back Bar of Chain

Row 1 return: Yo, draw through 1 lp on hook, *yo, draw through 2 lps on hook, rep from * until 1 lp rem on hook.

Row 2: *Sk next 2 sts, **tss** *(see page 8)*, tss in 2nd sk st, tss in first sk st, rep from * across until 1 st rem, tss under both strands of last st.

Row 2 return: Rep row 1 return.

Rep row 2 for desired length. Bind off in sl st. ∎

Shells & Vertical Lines

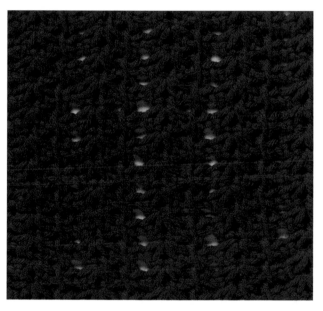

Multiple of 5 + 3

INSTRUCTIONS

Row 1: Ch desired number, working in **back bump** *(see illustration)* of chs, pick up a lp in 2nd ch from hook and in each rem ch across, leaving all lps on hook.

Back Bar of Chain

Row 1 return: Yo, draw through 1 lp, yo, draw through 2 lps, *ch 2, yo, draw through 5 lps, ch 2, yo, draw through 2 lps, rep from * across, ending with yo, draw through 2 lps.

Row 2: *Tss *(see page 8)* in next st, pick up lp in each of next 2 chs, sk next shell, pick up lp in each of next 2 chs, rep from * until 2 sts rem, tss in next st, tss under both strands of last st.

Row 2 return: Rep row 1 return.

Rep row 2 for desired length. Bind off in pattern. ■

Smocked Stitch

Multiple of any even number

PATTERN NOTES
When yarning over from front to back before doing **Tunisian purl stitch** (see page 9), yarn must be brought back to front. This adds a stitch on the hook to compensate for the decrease when you worked Tunisian purl stitch 2 stitches together.

The stitch count remains the same at end of each row.

SPECIAL STITCH
Tunisian purl stitch decrease (tps dec): Tps (see page 9) under next 2 vertical bars as one.

INSTRUCTIONS
Row 1: Ch desired number, working in **back bump** (see illustration) of chs, pick up a lp in 2nd ch from hook and in each rem ch across, leaving all lps on hook.

Back Bar of Chain

Row 1 return: Yo, draw through 1 lp on hook, *yo, draw through 2 lps on hook, rep from * until 1 lp rem on hook.

Row 2: Tps dec (see Special Stitch), *yo from front to back, tps dec, rep from * until 1 st rem, yo from back to front, **tss** (see page 8) under both strands of last st.

Row 2 return: Rep row 1 return.

Row 3: Sk next st, *yo from front to back, tps dec (this will include one st from each of 2 clusters from previous row), rep from * until 2 sts rem, yo from front to back, **tps** (see Pattern Notes) in next st, tss under both strands of last st.

Row 3 return: Rep row 1 return.

Rep rows 2 and 3 for desired length. Bind off in sl st. ■

Diagonal Lattice Stitch

Multiple of any odd number

INSTRUCTIONS

Row 1: Ch desired number, working in **back bump** *(see illustration)* of chs, pick up a lp in 2nd ch from hook and in each rem ch across, leaving all lps on hook.

Back Bar of Chain

Row 1 return: Yo, draw through 1 lp on hook, *yo, draw through 2 lps on hook, rep from * until 1 lp rem on hook.

Row 2: *Tss *(see page 8)* under next 2 vertical bars as 1, tss under first of these 2 bars, rep from * until 2 sts rem, tss under next st, tss under both strands of last st.

Row 2 return: Rep row 1 return.

Row 3: Tss under next st, *tss under next 2 vertical bars as 1, tss under first of these 2 bars, rep from * across, picking up under both strands of last st.

Row 3 return: Rep row 1 return.

Rep rows 2 and 3 for desired length. Bind off in pattern. ■

Encircled Stitches

Multiple of any even number

INSTRUCTIONS

Row 1: Ch desired number, working in **back bump** *(see illustration)* of chs, pick up a lp in 2nd ch from hook and in each rem ch across, leaving all lps on hook.

Back Bar of Chain

Row 1 return: Yo, draw through 1 lp on hook, *yo, draw through 2 lps on hook, rep from * until 1 lp rem on hook.

Row 2: Yo, 2 **tks** *(see page 8)*, draw last 2 lps on hook through yo as a group, *yo, 2 tks, draw last 2 lps on hook through yo as a group, rep from * until 1 st rem, **tss** *(see page 8)* under both strands of last st.

Row 2 return: Rep row 1 return.

Rep row 2 for desired length. Bind off in sl st as if to tss. ■

Comma Stitch

Multiple of any odd number

PATTERN NOTE
Stitches created by yarn overs will look diagonal rather than vertical on following row.

SPECIAL STITCH
Tunisian simple stitch decrease (tss dec): Tss (*see page 8*) under next 2 vertical bars as 1.

INSTRUCTIONS
Row 1: Ch desired number, working in **back bump** (*see illustration*) of chs, pick up a lp in 2nd ch from hook and in each rem ch across, leaving all lps on hook.

Back Bar of Chain

Row 1 return: Yo, draw through 1 lp on hook, *yo, draw through 2 lps on hook, rep from * until 1 lp rem on hook.

Row 2: *Tss dec (*see Special Stitch*), yo, rep from * until 2 sts rem, tss, tss under both strands of last st.

Row 2 return: Rep row 1 return.

Row 3: *Tss, pick up lp under top strand of next horizontal st, sk next st (*this is the st that looks diagonal*), rep from * across until 2 sts rem, tss, tss under both strands of last st.

Row 3 return: Rep row 1 return.

Rep rows 2 and 3 for desired length. Bind off in sl st. ■

Muscovite or Pebble Stitch

Multiple of 4

PATTERN NOTES
The pebbles are created by the additional chains worked during the return portion. Larger pebbles may be created using more chains.

Placement of pebbles can be altered as desired. However, this may alter the pattern repeat.

INSTRUCTIONS
Row 1: Ch desired number, working in **back bump** (*see illustration*) of chs, pick up a lp in

2nd ch from hook and in each rem ch across, leaving all lps on hook.

Back Bar of Chain

Row 1 return: Yo, draw through 1 lp on hook, *yo, draw through 2 lps on hook, rep from * until 1 lp rem on hook.

Row 2: Tss (*see page 8*) in each st across, working last tss under both strands of last st.

Row 2 return: Yo, draw through 1 lp on hook, [yo, draw through 2 lps on hook] 3 times, *ch 3, [yo, draw through 2 lps on hook] 4 times, rep from * until 1 lp rem on hook.

Row 3: Keeping ch-3 lps to front of work, tss in each st across, working last tss under both strands of last st.

Row 3 return: Yo, draw through 1 lp on hook, yo, draw through 2 lps on hook, *ch 3, [yo, draw through 2 lps on hook] 4 times, rep from * across, ending with ch 3, [yo, draw through 2 lps on hook] twice.

Rep rows 2 and 3 for desired length, ending after row 2 return. Bind off in sc. ■

Diagonal Eyelet Stitch

Multiple of 7 + 5

SPECIAL STITCH

Tunisian simple stitch decrease (tss dec): Tss (*see page 8*) under next 2 vertical bars as 1.

INSTRUCTIONS

Row 1: Ch desired number, working in **back bump** (*see illustration*) of chs, pick up a lp in 2nd ch from hook and in each rem ch across, leaving all lps on hook.

Back Bar of Chain

Row 1 return: Yo, draw through 1 lp on hook, *yo, draw through 2 lps on hook, rep from * until 1 lp rem on hook.

Row 2: *3 tss, [yo, **tss dec** *(see Special Stitch)*, ch 1] twice, rep from * across until 4 sts rem, 3 tss, tss under both strands of last st.

Row 2 return: Rep row 1 return.

Row 3: Tss, *3 tss, [yo, tss dec, ch 1] twice, rep from * across until 3 sts rem, 2 tss, tss under both strands of last st.

Row 3 return: Rep row 1 return.

Row 4: Yo, tss dec, ch 1, *3 tss, [yo, tss dec, ch 1] twice, rep from * across until 2 sts rem, tss, tss under both strands of last st.

Row 4 return: Rep row 1 return.

Row 5: Tss, yo, tss dec, ch 1, *3 tss, [yo, tss dec, ch 1] twice, rep from * across until 1 st rem, tss under both strands of last st.

Row 5 return: Rep row 1 return.

Row 6: [Yo, tss dec, ch 1] twice, *3 tss, [yo, tss dec, ch 1] twice, rep from * across until 7 sts rem, 3 tss, yo, tss dec, ch 1, tss, tss under both strands of last st.

Row 6 return: Rep row 1 return.

Row 7: Tss, [yo, tss dec, ch 1] twice, *3 tss, [yo, tss dec, ch 1] twice, rep from * across until 6 sts rem, 3 tss, yo, tss dec, ch 1, tss, tss under both strands of last st.

Row 7 return: Rep row 1 return.

Row 8: 2 tss, [yo, tss dec, ch 1] twice, *3 tss, [yo, tss dec, ch 1] twice, rep from * across until 5 sts rem, 4 tss, tss under both strands of last st.

Row 8 return: Rep row 1 return.

Rep rows 2–8 for desired length. Bind off in sl st as if to tss. ■

Basket Weave

Multiple of odd number divisible by 5 + 2

INSTRUCTIONS

Row 1: Ch desired number, working in **back bump** *(see illustration)* of chs, pick up a lp in 2nd ch from hook and in each rem ch across, leaving all lps on hook.

Back Bar of Chain

Row 1 return: Yo, draw through 1 lp on hook, *yo, draw through 2 lps on hook, rep from * until 1 lp rem on hook.

Row 2: Tps *(see page 9)* in each of next 5 sts, ***tks** *(see page 8)* in each of next 5 sts, tps in each of next 5 sts, rep from * until 1 st rem, **tss** *(see page 8)* under both strands of last st.

Row 2 return: Rep row 1 return.

Rows 3–5: Rep row 2.

Row 6: Tks in each of next 5 sts, *tps in each of next 5 sts, tks in each of next 5 sts, rep from * until 1 st rem, tss under both strands of last st.

Row 6 return: Rep row 1 return.

Rows 7–9: Rep row 6.

Rep rows 2–9 for desired length, ending with row 5. Bind off in sl st. ∎

Seed Stitch

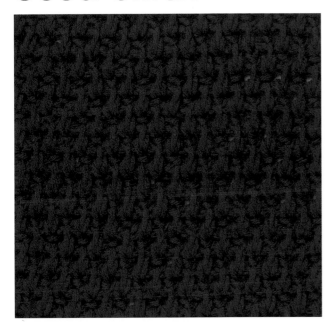

Multiple of any odd number

INSTRUCTIONS
Row 1: Ch desired number, working in **back bump** (*see illustration*) of chs, pick up a lp in 2nd ch from hook and in each rem ch across, leaving all lps on hook.

Back Bar of Chain

Row 1 return: Yo, draw through 1 lp on hook, *yo, draw through 2 lps on hook, rep from * until 1 lp rem on hook.

Row 2: *Tks (*see page 8*) in next st, tps in next st, rep from * across until 2 sts rem, tks in next st, tss (*see page 8*) under both strands of last st.

Row 2 return: Rep row 1 return.

Row 3: *Tps in next st, tks in next st, rep from * across until 2 sts rem, tps in next st, tss under both strands of last st.

Row 3 return: Rep row 1 return.

Rep rows 2 and 3 for desired length. Bind off in pattern. ∎

Cross-Stitch

Multiple of any number

INSTRUCTIONS
Row 1: Ch desired number, working in **back bump** (*see illustration*) of chs, pick up lp in 2nd ch from hook and in each rem ch across, leaving all lps on hook.

Back Bar of Chain

Row 1 return: Yo, draw through 1 lp on hook, *yo, draw through 2 lps on hook, rep from * until 1 lp rem on hook.

Row 2: *Sk next st, **tss** (*see page 8*) in next st, tss in sk st, rep from * across until 1 st rem, tss under both strands of last st.

Row 2 return: Rep row 1 return.

Rep row 2 for desired length. Bind off in sl st in pattern. ■

Shells & Horizontal Lines

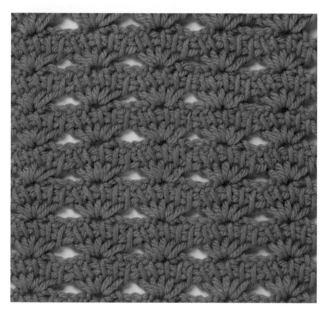

Multiple of 5 + 2

INSTRUCTIONS

Row 1: Ch desired number, working in **back bump** (*see illustration*) of chs, pick up a lp in 2nd ch from hook and in each rem ch across, leaving all lps on hook.

Back Bar of Chain

Row 1 return: Yo, draw through 1 lp, ch 2, yo, draw through 6 lps, *ch 4, yo, draw through 6 lps, rep from * until 2 lps rem on hook, ch 2, yo, draw through last 2 lps on hook.

Row 2: Pick up lp in each of next 2 chs, pick up lp in top of next shell, pick up lp in each of next 4 chs, rep from * across, ending pick up lp in each of last 2 chs, **tss** (*see page 8*) under both strands of last st.

Row 2 return: Yo, draw through 1 lp on hook, *yo, draw through 2 lps on hook, rep from * across until 1 lp rem.

Row 3: Tss in each st across, picking up under both strands of last st.

Row 3 return: Rep row 1 return.

Rep rows 2 and 3 for desired length, ending with row 2 return. Bind off in sl st. ■

Lacy Shells

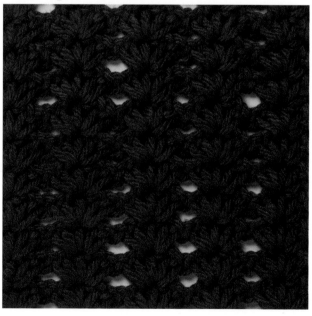

Multiple of 5 + 2 sts

INSTRUCTIONS

Row 1: Ch desired number, working in **back bump** (*see illustration*) of chs, pick up a lp in 2nd ch from hook and in each rem ch across, leaving all lps on hook.

Back Bar of Chain

Row 1 return: Yo, draw through 1 lp, ch 2, yo, draw through 6 lps on hook, *ch 4, yo, draw through 6 lps on hook, rep from * until 2 lps rem on hook, ch 2, yo, draw through last 2 lps on hook.

Row 2: Pick up lp in each of next 2 chs, *pick up lp in top of next shell, pick up lp in each of next 4 chs, rep from * across, ending pick up lp in each of last 2 chs, **tss** (*see page 8*) under both strands of last st.

Row 2 return: Rep row 1 return.

Rep row 2 for desired length. Bind off in sl st. ∎

Chained Cable

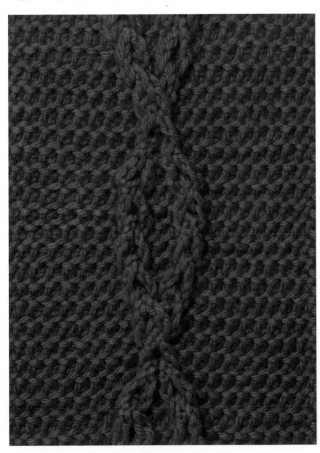

Multiple of 6 + minimum of 2 for edge sts (exact number will depend on how many sts on each side of cable)

PATTERN NOTE
Shown here against a background of **Tunisian purl stitch** (*see page 9*), the cables may also be worked on Tunisian simple stitch or Tunisian knit stitch background.

INSTRUCTIONS
Row 1: Ch desired number, working in **back bump** (*see illustration*) of chs, pick up a lp in 2nd ch from hook and in each rem ch across, leaving all lps on hook.

Back Bar of Chain

Row 1 return: *Yo, draw through 2 lps on hook, rep from * until 1 lp rem on hook.

Row 2: *Tps (*see page 9*) in next st, rep from * until you reach point where first leg of cable is desired, ch 7, remove lp from hook, insert hook through last tps worked, place lp back on hook and draw through, tps in each of next 4 sts, ch 7, remove lp from hook, insert hook through last tps worked, place lp back on hook and draw through, rep from * across until 1 st rem, **tss** (*see page 8*) under both strands of last st.

Row 2 return: Rep row 1 return, keeping ch-7 lps to front of work.

Row 3: Tps in each st across until 1 st rem, tss under both strands of last st.

Row 3 return: Rep row 1 return.

Rows 4 and 5: Rep rows 2 and 3.

Row 6: Tps in each st until 1 st past first leg of cable, ch 7, remove lp from hook, insert hook through last tps worked, place lp back on hook and draw through, 2 tps, ch 7, remove lp from hook, insert hook through last tps worked, place lp back on hook and draw through, tps until 1 st rem, tss under both lps of last st.

Row 6 return: Rep row 1 return, making sure ch-7 lps stay to front of work.

Row 7: Rep row 3.

Row 8: Tps in each st until 2 sts past original first leg of cable, ch 7, remove lp from hook, insert hook through last tps worked, place lp back on hook and draw through, tps until 1 st rem, tss under both lps of last st.

Row 8 return: Rep row 1 return, making sure ch-7 lp stays to front of work.

Row 9: Rep row 3.

Row 10: Rep row 6.

Row 11: Rep row 3.

Rows 12–15: Rep rows 2–5.

Rows 16 & 17: Rep rows 2 and 3.

Rows 18–21: Rep rows 8–11.

Rows 22 & 23: Rep rows 8 and 9.

Rows 24 & 25: Rep rows 2 and 3.

Rep rows 4–25 until 1 row before desired length.

Interlace ch lps, drawing each successive ch lp through ch lp below it, at point where there is only 1 ch lp, pull ch lp through both of previous ch lps at same time, then pull both of ch lps above through same lp and continue. After lacing all ch lps, place last 2 ch lps on locking stitch markers.

Next row: *Tps in each st across until ch lp is reached, insert hook through ch lp, yo and draw through lp and 1 lp on hook, securing ch lp, rep from * across, working tss under both strands of last st.

Next row return: Rep row 1 return. Bind off in sl st. ∎

Eyelets & Columns

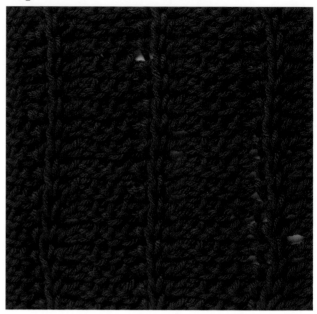

Multiple of 6 + 3

INSTRUCTIONS

Row 1: Ch desired number, working in **back bump** (*see illustration*) of chs, pick up a lp in 2nd ch from hook and in each rem ch across, leaving all lps on hook.

Back Bar of Chain

Row 1 return: *Yo, draw through 2 lps on hook, rep from * until 1 lp rem on hook.

Row 2: 2 **tps** (*see page 9*), *yo from back to front, sk next st, **tks** (*see page 8*), yo from front to back, sk next st, 3 tps, rep from * across, ending last rep with 2 tps, **tss** (*see page 8*) under both strands of last st.

Row 2 return: Rep row 1 return.

Rep row 2 for desired length. Bind off in sl st as if to tss. ∎

Satin Stitches & Vs

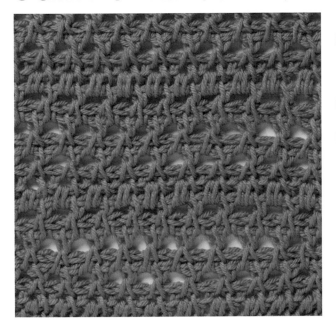

Multiple of any even number

PATTERN NOTES
Stitches created by yarn overs will look diagonal, rather than vertical, on following row.

SPECIAL STITCH
Tunisian simple stitch decrease (tss dec): Tss *(see page 8)* under next 2 vertical bars as one.

INSTRUCTIONS
Row 1: Ch desired number, working in **back bump** *(see illustration)* of chs, pick up a lp in 2nd ch from hook and in each rem ch across, leaving all lps on hook.

Back Bar of Chain

Row 1 return: Yo, draw through 1 lp on hook, *yo, draw through 2 lps on hook, rep from * until 1 lp rem on hook.

Row 2: *Tss dec *(see Special Stitch)*, yo, rep from * across until 1 st rem, tss under both strands of last st.

Row 2 return: Rep row 1 return.

Row 3: Tss, *(tss, yo, tss) in next st, tss, rep from * across until 1 st rem, tss under both strands of last st. *([original number minus 1] x 2)*

Row 3 return: Yo, draw through 1 lp on hook *yo, draw through 4 lps on hook, yo, draw through 2 lps on hook, rep from * across until 2 lps rem on hook, yo, draw through last 2 lps.

Row 4: *Tss, pick up lp under horizontal bar at top of next cluster, rep from * across until 1 st rem, tss under both strands of last st.

Row 4 return: Rep row 1 return.

Row 5: Rep row 2.

Row 6: *Tss, **tks** *(see page 8)*, rep from * across until 1 st rem, tss under both strands of last st.

Row 6 return: Rep row 1 return.

Row 7: *Yo, tss dec, rep from * across until 1 st rem, tss under both strands of last st.

Row 7 return: Rep row 1 return.

Row 8: *Tks, tss, rep from * across until 1 st rem, tss under both strands of last st.

Row 8 return: Rep row 1 return.

Rep rows 2–8 for desired length. Bind-off in sl st as if to tss. ■

Slender Shells

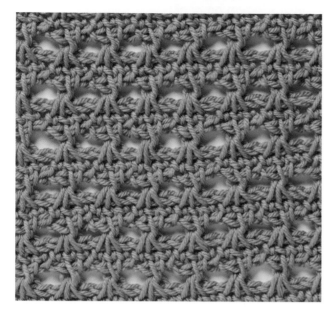

Multiple of any even number

PATTERN NOTES
Stitches created by yarn overs will look diagonal, rather than vertical, on following row. They can be a bit difficult to spot, particularly when there is a double yarn over.

SPECIAL STITCH
Tunisian simple stitch decrease (tss dec): Tss (*see page 8*) under next 3 vertical bars as 1.

INSTRUCTIONS
Row 1: Ch desired number, working in **back bump** (*see illustration*) of chs, ch 1, *pick up lp in next ch, ch 1, rep from * across, leaving all lps on hook.

Back Bar of Chain

Row 1 return: Yo, draw through 1 lp on hook, *yo, draw through 2 lps on hook, rep from * until 1 lp rem on hook.

Row 2: *Yo, **tss dec** (*see Special Stitch*), yo, rep from * until 1 st rem, tss under both strands of last st.

Row 2 return: Yo, draw through 1 lp on hook, *yo, draw through 2 lps on hook, rep from * across until 1 lp rem on hook.

Row 3: Extss (see page 10) in each st across until 1 st rem, tss under both strands of last st.

Row 3 return: Rep row 1 return.

Rep rows 2 and 3 for desired length, ending with row 2 return. Bind off in sl st. ■

Chevron Ripple

Multiple of 16 + 2

INSTRUCTIONS
Row 1: Ch desired number, working in **back bump** (*see illustration*) of chs, pick up a lp in 2nd ch from hook and in each rem ch across, leaving all lps on hook.

Back Bar of Chain

Row 1 return: Yo, draw through 3 lps, *[yo, draw through 2 lps on hook] 6 times, ch 2, [yo, draw through 2 lps on hook] 6 times, yo, draw through 5 lps on hook, rep from * across, ending last rep with yo, draw through 4 lps on hook.

Row 2: Ch 1, *sk next cluster, 6 **extss** (*see page 10*), [pick up lp in next ch-2 sp, ch 1] 4 times, 6 extss, rep from * across until 1 cluster rem, pick up lp in top of last cluster, ch 1.

Row 2 return: Rep row 1 return.

Rep row 2 for desired length.

Bind off row: Ch 1, *sk next cluster, [extss, draw through lp on hook] 6 times, [pick up lp in next ch-2 sp, ch 1, draw through lp on hook] 4 times, [extss, draw through lp on hook] 6 times, rep from * across, ending pick up lp in top of last cluster, draw through lp on hook. ■

Eyelet Stitch

Multiple of any odd number

INSTRUCTIONS
Row 1: Ch desired number, working in **back bump** (*see illustration*) of chs, pick up a lp in

2nd ch from hook and in each rem ch across, leaving all lps on hook.

Back Bar of Chain

Row 1 return: Yo, draw through 1 lp on hook, *yo, draw through 2 lps on hook, rep from * until 1 lp rem on hook.

Row 2: *Yo, sk next st, **tss** (*see page 8*), rep from * across, ending tss under both strands of last st.

Row 2 return: Rep row 1 return.

Rep row 2 for desired length. Bind off in sl st as if to tss. ■

Columns

Multiple of 5

INSTRUCTIONS
Row 1: Ch desired number, working in **back bump** (*see illustration*) of chs, pick up a lp in 2nd ch from hook and in each rem ch across, leaving all lps on hook.

Back Bar of Chain

Back Bar of Chain

Row 1 return: Yo, draw through 1 lp on hook, *yo, draw through 2 lps on hook, rep from * until 1 lp rem on hook.

Row 2: ***Tss** (*see page 8*), **tps** (*see page 9*), tss, 2 **tks** (*see page 8*), rep from * across until 4 sts rem, tss, tps, tss, tss under both strands of last st.

Row 2 return: Rep row 1 return.

Rep row 2 for desired length. Bind off in sl st. ∎

Honeycomb Stitch (aka Moss Stitch)

Row 1 return: Yo, draw through 1 lp on hook, *yo, draw through 2 lps on hook, rep from * until 1 lp rem on hook.

Row 2: ***Tss** (*see page 8*) in next st, **tps** (*see page 9*) in next st, rep from * until 2 sts rem, tss in next st, tss under both strands of last st.

Row 2 return: Rep row 1 return.

Row 3: *Tps in next st, tss in next st, rep from * until 2 sts rem, tps in next st, tss under both strands of last st.

Row 3 return: Rep row 1 return.

Rep rows 2 and 3 for desired length. Bind off in pattern. ∎

Clove Stitch

Multiple of any odd number

INSTRUCTIONS
Row 1: Ch desired number, working in **back bump** (*see illustration*) of chs, pick up a lp in 2nd ch from hook and in each rem ch across, leaving all lps on hook.

Multiple of any odd number

PATTERN NOTE
When picking up lp to left of diagonal strand

(*yarn over stitch from previous row*), insert hook in space. In other words, insert hook under horizontal connecting stitches as when working **Tunisian full stitch** (*see page 12*).

INSTRUCTIONS

Row 1: Ch desired number, yo, working in **back bump** (*see illustration*) of chs, pick up a lp in 2nd ch from hook, yo and draw through 3 lps on hook, *yo, sk next ch, pick up lp in next ch, yo, pick up lp in same ch, yo and draw through 3 lps on hook, rep from * across until 1 ch rem, yo, pick up lp in last ch, ch 1. (*same number of sts as beg ch*)

Back Bar of Chain

Row 1 return: *Yo, draw through 2 lps on hook, rep from * across until 1 lp rem on hook.

Row 2: Ch 1, *yo, pick up lp in sp to left of next diagonal strand, yo, pick up lp in same sp, yo, draw through 3 lps on hook, rep from * across until 1 st rem, **tss** (*see page 8*) under both strands of last st, ch 1. (*original number of sts + 1 lp on hook*)

Row 2 return: Rep row 1 return.

Row 3: Ch 1, yo, pick up lp in sp to left of first diagonal strand, yo, draw through 3 lps on hook, *yo, pick up lp in sp to left of next diagonal strand, yo, pick up lp in same sp, yo draw through 3 lps on hook, rep from * across until 1 st rem, yo, tss under both strands of last st, ch 1. (*same number of sts as beg ch*)

Row 3 return: Rep row 1 return.

Rep rows 2 and 3 for desired length. Bind off in sl st. ■

Little Bobbles in a Row

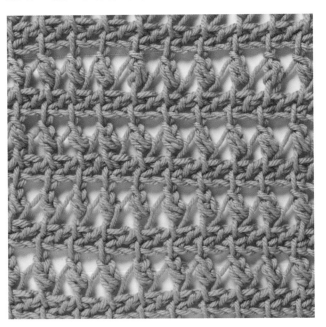

Multiple of any odd number

INSTRUCTIONS

Row 1: Ch desired number, working in **back bump** (*see illustration*) of chs, pick up a lp in 2nd ch from hook and in each rem ch across, leaving all lps on hook.

Back Bar of Chain

Row 1 return: Yo, draw through 1 lp on hook, *yo, draw through 2 lps on hook, rep from * until 1 lp rem on hook.

Row 2: Ch 3, *(**tss**—see page 8, yo, tss) in next st, yo, draw through 3 lps on hook, ch 1, sk next st, rep from * across until 2 sts rem, (tss, yo, tss) in next st, yo, draw through 3 lps, ch 1, tss under both strands of last st, ch 2. (*Number of lps on hook will be original ch minus 1 divided by 2 plus 2*)

Row 2 return: Yo, draw through 1 lp on hook, *yo, draw through 2 lps on hook, ch 1, rep from * across until 3 lps rem, [yo, draw through 2 lps] twice.

Row 3: *Tss in next st, pick up lp under top strand of next ch, rep from * across until 2 sts rem, tss, tss under both strands of last ch at end of previous row. *(Number of lps on hook will be original number of chs)*

Row 3 return: Rep row 1 return.

Rep rows 2 and 3 for desired length, ending with row 2 return. Bind off in sc, working in each st and ch across. ■

Feather & Fan Ripple

Multiple of 11 + 2

SPECIAL STITCHES

Tunisian simple stitch decrease (tss dec): Tss *(see page 8)* under next 2 vertical bars as 1.

Slip stitch decrease (sl st dec): Sl st in next 2 sts at same time.

INSTRUCTIONS

Row 1: Ch desired number, working in **back bump** *(see illustration)* of chs, pick up a lp in 2nd ch from hook and in each rem ch across, leaving all lps on hook.

Back Bar of Chain

Row 1 return: Yo, draw through 1 lp on hook, *yo, draw through 2 lps on hook, rep from * until 1 lp rem on hook.

Row 2: *[**Tss dec**—*see Special Stitches*] twice, [yo, **tks**—*see page 8*] 3 times, yo, [tss dec] twice, rep from * across until 1 st rem, tss under both strands of last st.

Row 2 return: Rep row 1 return.

Rep row 2 for desired length.

Bind-off row: *[**Sl st dec** *(see Special Stitches)* as if to tss] twice, [ch 1, sl st as if to tks] 3 times, ch 1, [sl st dec as if to tss] twice, rep from * across, ending with sl st as if to tss under both strands of last st. ■

Alternating Cross-Stitch

Multiple of any number

INSTRUCTIONS

Row 1: Ch desired number, working in **back bump** *(see illustration)* of chs, pick up a lp in 2nd ch from hook and in each rem ch across, leaving all lps on hook.

Back Bar of Chain

Row 1 return: Yo, draw through 1 lp on hook, *yo, draw through 2 lps on hook, rep from * until 1 lp rem on hook.

Row 2: *Sk next st, **tss** *(see page 8)* in next st, tss in sk st, rep from * across until 1 st rem, tss under both strands of last st.

Row 2 return: Rep row 1 return.

Row 3: Tss, *sk next st, tss in next st, tss in sk st, rep from * across until 2 sts rem, tss, tss under both strands of last st.

Row 3 return: Rep row 1 return.

Rep rows 2 and 3 for desired length. Bind off in sl st in pattern. ■

Tricolor Tweed

Multiple of any number

PATTERN NOTES

You will notice a much different look depending upon where additional colors are introduced in Tunisian crochet. Changing color at the beginning of a return portion of a row (in other words, the left edge) results in a woven or tweed effect. In order to create a stable left edge, the color being dropped must be "locked in." The following instructions will guide you through how to do that and how to carry unused color(s) neatly along the left edge. When picking up a previously dropped color, always pick it up from underneath current color.

Tunisian simple stitch *(see page 8)* was used for this swatch, but any stitch could be used.

INSTRUCTIONS

Row 1: With A, ch desired number, working in **back bump** *(see illustration)* of chs, pick up a lp in 2nd ch from hook and in each rem ch across, leaving all lps on hook.

Back Bar of Chain

Row 1 return: Drape A over hook from front to back to left of sts, draw B through first lp on hook, yo, draw through 2 lps on hook *(this locks dropped color in place),* *yo, draw through 2 lps on hook, rep from * across until 1 lp rem on hook.

Row 2: Tss *(see page 8)* in each st across until 1 st rem, tss under both strands of last st.

Row 2 return: Drape A and B over hook from front to back to left of sts, draw C through first lp on hook, yo, draw through 2 lps on hook *(this locks dropped color in place),* *yo, draw through 2 lps on hook, rep from * across until 1 lp rem on hook.

Row 3: Tss in each st across until 1 st rem, tss under both strands of last st.

Row 3 return: Drape B and C over hook from front to back to left of sts, pick up A from underneath C, yo, draw through first lp on hook, *yo, draw through 2 lps on hook, rep from * across until 1 lp rem on hook.

Rep row 3, working A, B and C in sequence and carrying unused colors up left edge. Bind off in sl st. ■

Tricolor Stripe

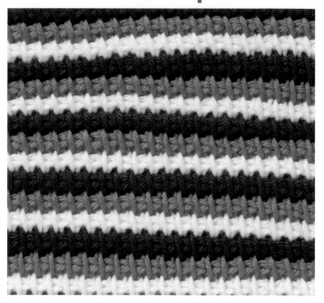

Multiple of any number

PATTERN NOTES

You will notice a much different look depending upon where you introduce additional colors in Tunisian crochet. Changing color at the beginning of the forward pass of a row (in other words, the right edge) results in solid stripes. Because the first stitch of the row actually happens with the last action of return pass, that is where you will change colors. The following instructions will guide you through how to do that and how to carry the unused color(s) neatly along the right edge in order to avoid long floats. When picking up a previously dropped color, always pick it up from underneath the current color.

Tunisian simple stitch *(see page 8)* was used for this swatch, but any stitch could be used.

INSTRUCTIONS

Row 1: With A, ch desired number, working in **back bump** *(see illustration)* of chs, pick up a lp in 2nd ch from hook and in each rem ch across, leaving all lps on hook.

Back Bar of Chain

Row 1 return: Yo, draw through 1 lp on hook, *yo, draw through 2 lps on hook, rep from * across until 2 lps rem, with B, yo, draw through last 2 lps.

Row 2: Before beg, lock dropped color in place by bringing it up from WS and lay it across working yarn below hook to left of lp on hook, **tss** (*see page 8*) in each st across until 1 st rem, tss under both strands of last st.

Row 2 return: Yo, draw through 1 lp on hook, *yo, draw through 2 lps on hook, rep from * across until 2 lps rem on hook, with C, yo, draw through last 2 lps.

Row 3: Before beg, lock dropped colors in place by bringing both colors up from wrong side and lay them across working yarn below hook to left of lp on hook, tss in each st across until 1 st rem, tss under both strands of last st.

Row 3 return: Yo, draw through 1 lp on hook, *yo, draw through 2 lps on hook, rep from * across until 2 lps rem, with A, yo, draw through last 2 lps.

Rep row 3, working A, B and C in sequence and carrying unused colors up right edge. Bind off in sl st. ∎

Hopscotch

Multiple of 3 + 1

PATTERN NOTE

For most post stitches, if instructions don't specify, you can work either front vertical bar as if to **Tunisian simple stitch** (*see page 8*) or around the entire stitch, as if working a front post stitch in classic crochet. Be sure to be consistent within project.

SPECIAL STITCH

Front post Tunisian double stitch (fptds): Yo, insert hook in designated st, yo, draw up a lp, yo, draw through 2 lps on hook, drawing lp rem on hook up to height of current row. On current row, sk st directly behind fptds.

INSTRUCTIONS

Row 1: With A, ch desired number, working in **back bump** (*see illustration*) of chs, pick up a lp in 2nd ch from hook and in each rem ch across, leaving all lps on hook.

Back Bar of Chain

Row 1 return: Yo, draw through 1 lp on hook, *yo, draw through 2 lps on hook, rep from * until 1 lp rem on hook.

Row 2: **Tss** *(see page 8)* in each st across, working last tss under both strands of last st.

Row 2 return: Yo, draw through 1 lp on hook, *yo, draw through 2 lps on hook, rep from * across until 2 lps rem on hook, with B, yo, draw through last 2 lps.

Row 3: With B, *2 tss, **fptds** *(see Special Stitch)* around both strands of st 2 rows below, rep from * across until 3 sts rem, 2 tss, tss under both strands of last st.

Row 3 return: Rep row 1 return.

Row 4: Tss in each st across, working last tss under both strands of last st.

Row 4 return: Yo, draw through 1 lp on hook, *yo, draw through 2 lps on hook, rep from * across until 2 lps rem on hook, with A, yo, draw through last 2 lps.

Row 5: With A, rep row 3.

Rep Rows 2–5 for desired length, ending with row 2 return, but do not change color. With A, bind off in sl st as if to tss. ■

Trinity

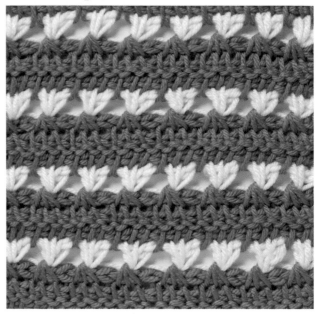

Multiple of 3 + 2

SPECIAL STITCH
Tunisian simple stitch decrease (tss dec): Tss *(see page 8)* under next 3 vertical bars as one.

INSTRUCTIONS
Row 1: With A, ch desired number, working in **back bump** *(see illustration)* of chs, pick up a lp in 2nd ch from hook and in each rem ch across, leaving all lps on hook.

Back Bar of Chain

Row 1 return: Yo, draw through 1 lp on hook, *yo, draw through 2 lps on hook, rep from * across until 2 lps rem, with B, yo, draw through last 2 lps.

Row 2: With B, *tss dec *(see Special Stitch)*, yo, tss dec in same 3 sts, rep from * across until 1 st rem, tss under both strands of last st.

Row 2 return: With B, rep row 1 return, changing to A with the last 2 lps.

Row 3: *With A, tss, sk next st, tss, **tfs** *(see page 12)*, rep from * across until 1 st rem, tss under both strands of last st.

Row 3 return: Yo, draw through 1 lp on hook, *yo, draw through 2 lps on hook, rep from * until 1 lp rem on hook.

Row 4: With A, **tps** *(see page 9)* in each st across until 1 st rem, tss under both strands of last st.

Row 4 return: Rep row 3 return.

Row 5: With A, tss in each st across until 1 st rem, tss under both strands of last st.

Row 5 return: Rep row 1 return.

Rep rows 2–5 for desired length, ending with row 3 return. With A, bind off in sl st as if to tss. ∎

Blocks

Multiple of 4 + 3

PATTERN NOTE
For most post sts, if instructions don't specify, you can work either front vertical bar as if to **tss** *(see page 8)* or around the entire st, as if working a front post stitch in classic crochet.

Be sure to be consistent within the project. In photograph, post st was worked under front vertical bar as if to tss.

SPECIAL STITCH
Front post extended Tunisian double stitch (fpextds): Yo, insert hook in designated st, yo, draw up a lp, yo, draw through 1 lp on hook, yo, draw through 2 lps on hook, drawing lp rem on hook up to height of current row. On current row, sk st directly behind fpextds.

INSTRUCTIONS
Row 1: With A, ch desired number, working in **back bump** *(see illustration)* of chs, pick up a lp in 2nd ch from hook and in each rem ch across, leaving all lps on hook.

Back Bar of Chain

Row 1 return: Yo, draw through 1 lp on hook, *yo, draw through 2 lps on hook, rep from * until 2 lps rem, with B, yo, draw through last 2 lps.

Row 2: Tss in each st across, working last tss under both strands of last st.

Row 2 return: Yo, draw through 1 lp on hook, *yo, draw through 2 lps on hook, rep from * across until 1 lp rem on hook.

Row 3: Tps *(see page 9)* in each st across until 1 st rem, tss under both strands of last st.

Row 3 return: Rep row 1 return, changing to A with the last 2 lps.

Row 4: 2 tss, *fpextdc *(see Special Stitch)* in next st 3 rows below *(row of same color)*, 3 tss, rep from * across, working last tss under both strands of last st.

Row 4 return: Rep row 1 return.

Rep rows 2–4 for desired length, ending with row 4 return, but do not change color.

With A, bind off in sl st as if to tss. ∎

Simple Slips

Multiple of any odd number

SPECIAL STITCH

Slip 1 without working (sl 1 wow): Insert hook under next vertical bar, keeping this strand on hook continue. (*This is an easy way to have 2 colors, appear in a row while working with 1 color at a time.*)

INSTRUCTIONS

Row 1: With A, ch desired number, working in **back bump** (*see illustration*) of chs, pick up a lp in 2nd ch from hook and in each rem ch across, leaving all lps on hook.

Back Bar of Chain

Row 1 return: Yo, draw through 1 lp on hook, *yo, draw through 2 lps on hook, rep from * until 2 lps rem on hook, with B, yo, draw through last 2 lps.

Row 2: *Sl 1 wow (*see Special Stitch*), with B, pick up lp in horizontal bar at top and slightly behind next st, rep from * across until 1 st rem, **tss** (*see page 8*) under both strands of last st.

Row 2 return: With B, rep row 1 return, changing to A with last 2 lps.

Row 3: *With A, pick up lp in horizontal bar at top and slightly behind next st, sl 1 wow, rep from * across until 1 st rem, tss under both strands of last st.

Row 3 return: Rep row 1 return.

Rep rows 2 and 3 for desired length, ending with row 2 return. With A, bind off in pattern with sc. ■

Waves

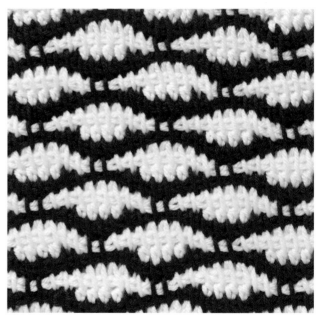

Multiple of 10

SPECIAL STITCH

Slip 2 without working (sl 2 wow): [Insert hook under next vertical bar, keeping this strand on hook] twice. (*This is an easy way to have 2 colors appear in a row while working with 1 color at a time.*)

INSTRUCTIONS

Row 1: With A, ch desired number, working in **back bump** (*see illustration*) of chs, pick up a lp in 2nd ch from hook and in each rem ch across, leaving all lps on hook.

Back Bar of Chain

Row 1 return: Yo, draw through 1 lp on hook, *yo, draw through 2 lps on hook, rep from * until 2 lps rem on hook, with B, yo, draw through last 2 lps.

Row 2: With B, *2 **tss** (*see page 8*), 4 **tds** (*see page 11*), 2 tss, **sl 2 wow** (*see Special Stitch*), rep from * across until 3 sts rem, 2 tss, tss under both strands of last st.

Row 2 return: With B, rep row 1 return, changing to A with last 2 lps.

Row 3: With A, tss in each st across until 1 st rem, tss under both strands of last st.

Row 3 return: Rep row 1 return.

Row 4: With B, ch 1, tds, *2 tss, sl 2 wow, 2 tss, 4 tds, rep from * across, ending last rep with tds, tds under both strands of last st.

Row 4 return: With B, rep row 1 return, changing to A with last 2 lps.

Row 5: Rep row 3.

Rep Rows 2–5 for desired length, ending with row 3 return, but do not change color. With A, bind off in sl st as if to tss. ∎

Houndstooth

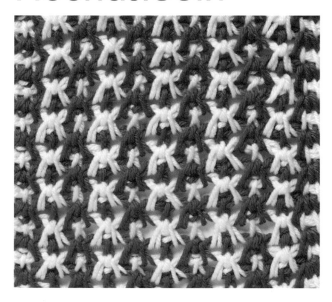

Multiple of 4 + 1

INSTRUCTIONS

Row 1: With A, ch desired number, working in **back bump** (*see illustration*) of chs, pick up a lp in 2nd ch from hook and in each rem ch across, leaving all lps on hook.

Back Bar of Chain

Row 1 return: Yo, draw through 1 lp on hook, *ch 1, yo, draw through 4 lps on hook, ch 1, yo, draw through 2 lps on hook, rep from * across until 2 lps rem on hook, with B, yo, draw through last 2 lps.

Row 2: With B, *tfs (*see page 12*), pick up lp in top of next cluster, tfs, tps, rep from * across until 1 cluster rem, tfs, pick up lp in top of cluster, tfs, **tss** (*see page 8*) under both strands of last st.

Row 2 return: Yo, draw through 1 lp on hook, [yo, draw through 2 lps on hook] twice, *ch 1, yo, draw through 4 lps on hook, ch 1, yo, draw through 2 lps on hook, rep from * across until 3 lps rem on hook, yo, draw through 2 lps on hook, with A, yo, draw through last 2 lps.

Row 3: With A, 2 tss, *tfs, pick up lp in top of next cluster, tfs, **tps** (*see page 9*), rep from * across until 2 sts rem, tss, tss under both strands of last st.

Row 3 return: Rep row 1 return.

Rep rows 2 and 3 for desired length, ending with row 3 return, but do not change color. With A, bind off in sl st in pattern. ■

Quotes

Multiple of 4

SPECIAL STITCH
Slip 2 without working (sl 2 wow): [Insert hook under next vertical bar, keeping this strand on hook] twice. (*This is an easy way to have 2 colors appear in a row while working with 1 color at a time.*)

INSTRUCTIONS
Row 1: With A, ch desired number, working in **back bump** (*see illustration*) of chs, pick up a lp in 2nd ch from hook and in each rem ch across, leaving all lps on hook.

Back Bar of Chain

Row 1 return: Draw B through first lp on hook, *yo, draw through 2 lps on hook, rep from * across until 1 lp rem on hook.

Row 2: ***Sl 2 wow** (*see Special Stitch*), 2 **ttws** (*see page 12*), rep from * across until 3 sts rem, sl 2 wow, **tss** (*see page 8*) under both strands of last st.

Row 2 return: With A, rep row 1 return.

Row 3: *2 tss, sl 2 wow, rep from * across until 3 sts rem, 2 tss, tss under both strands of last st.

Row 3 return: Yo, draw through 1 lp on hook, *yo, draw through 2 lps on hook, rep from * across until 1 lp rem on hook.

Row 4: *2 tss, 2 ttws, rep from * across until 3 sts rem, 2 tss, tss under both strands of last st.

Row 4 return: With B, yo draw through 1 lp on hook, *yo, draw through 2 lps on hook, rep from * across until 1 lp rem on hook.

Row 5: *2 ttws, sl 2 wow, rep from * across until 3 sts rem, 2 ttws, tss under both strands of last st.

Row 5 return: With A, yo, draw through 1 lp on hook, *yo, draw through 2 lps on hook, rep from * across until 1 lp rem on hook.

Row 6: *Sl 2 wow, 2 tss, rep from * across until 3 sts rem, sl 2 wow, tss under both strands of last st.

Row 6 return: Rep row 3 return.

Row 7: *2 ttws, 2 tss, rep from * across until 3 sts rem, 2 ttws, tss under both strands of last st.

Row 7 return: Rep row 4 return.

Rep rows 2–7 for desired length, ending with row 3 return. With A, bind off in sl st. ■

Fans

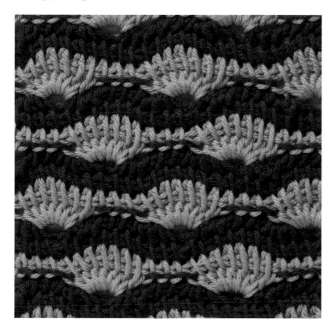

Multiple of 10 + 3

INSTRUCTIONS

Row 1: Ch desired number, working in **back bump** *(see illustration)* of chs, pick up a lp in 2nd ch from hook and in each rem ch across, leaving all lps on hook.

Back Bar of Chain

Row 1 return: Yo, draw through 1 lp on hook, *yo, draw through 2 lps on hook, rep from * across until 2 lps rem, with B, yo, draw through last 2 lps.

Row 2: With B, **tps** *(see page 9)*, *sk next 3 sts, 7 **tds** *(see page 11)* as if to **tks** *(see page 8)* in next st, sk next 3 sts, 3 tps, rep from * across until 1 st rem, **tss** *(see page 8)* under both strands of last st.

Row 2 return: Rep row 1 return, changing to A at end.

Row 3: With A, tss across until 1 st rem, tss under both strands of last st.

Row 3 return: Yo, draw through 1 lp on hook, * yo, draw through 2 lps on hook, rep from * across until 1 lp rem on hook.

Row 4: Rep row 3.

Row 4 return: Rep row 1 return.

Row 5: With B, 4 tds as if to tks in next st, sk next 3 sts, *3 tps, sk next 3 sts, 7 tds as if to tks in next st, sk next 3 sts, rep from * across until 2 sts rem, 4 tds as if to tks in next st, tss under both strands of last st.

Row 5 return: Rep row 1 return, changing to A at end.

Rows 6 & 7: Rep rows 3 and 4.

Rep rows 2–7 for desired length, ending after either row 3 or row 6 return. With A, bind off in sl st. ∎

Bricks

Multiple of 4 + 3

PATTERN NOTES

For most post stitches, if instructions don't specify, you can work either front vertical bar as if to **Tunisian simple stitch** (*see page 8*), or you can work around the entire stitch as if working a front post stitch in classic crochet. Be sure to be consistent within the project. As shown in photo, post stitch was worked around entire stitch.

SPECIAL STITCH

Front post extended tunisian double stitch (fpextds): Yo, insert hook in designated st, yo, draw up a lp, yo, draw through 1 lp on hook, yo, draw through 2 lps on hook, drawing lp rem on hook up to height of current row. On current row, sk st directly behind fpextds.

INSTRUCTIONS

Row 1: With A, ch desired number, working in **back bump** (*see illustration*) of chs, pick up a lp in 2nd ch from hook and in each rem ch across, leaving all lps on hook.

Back Bar of Chain

Row 1 return: Yo, draw through 1 lp on hook, *yo, draw through 2 lps on hook, rep from * until 2 lps rem, with B, yo, draw through last 2 lps.

Row 2: Tss (*see page 8*) in each st across, working last tss under both strands of last st.

Row 2 return: Yo, draw through 1 lp on hook, *yo, draw through 2 lps on hook, rep from * across until 1 lp rem on hook.

Row 2 return: Yo, draw through 1 lp on hook, *yo, draw through 2 lps on hook, rep from * across until 1 lp rem on hook.

Row 3: Tps (*see page 9*) in each st across until 1 st rem, tss under both strands of last st.

Row 3 return: Rep row 1 return, changing to A with last 2 lps.

Row 4: *Fpextds (*see Special Stitch*) in next st 3 rows below (*row of same color*), 3 tss, rep from * across, until 2 sts rem, fpextds in next st 3 rows below, tss under both strands of last st.

Row 4 return: Rep row 1 return.

Rows 5 & 6: Rep rows 2 and 3.

Row 7: 2 tss, *fpextds in next st 3 rows below (*row of same color*), 3 tss, rep from * across until 1 st rem, tss under both strands of last st.

Row 7 return: Rep row 1 return.

Rep rows 2–7 for desired length, ending with row 4 return, but do not change color. With A, bind off in sl st as if to tss. ■

Carats

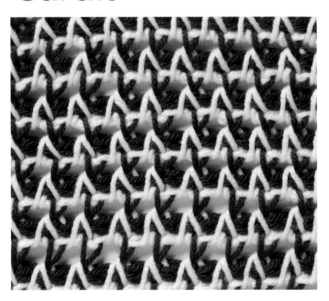

Multiple of any even number

SPECIAL STITCH

Tunisian simple stitch decrease (tss dec): Tss (*see page 8*) under next 2 vertical bars as 1.

INSTRUCTIONS

Row 1: With A, ch desired number, working in **back bump** (*see illustration*) of chs, pick up a lp in 2nd ch from hook and in each rem ch across, leaving all lps on hook.

Back Bar of Chain

Row 1 return: Yo, draw through 1 lp on hook, *yo, draw through 2 lps on hook, rep from * until 1 lp rem on hook.

Row 2: *Tss dec *(see Special Stitch)*, rep from * across until 1 st rem, tss under both strands of last st. *(number of sts on hook is ½ original number + 1)*

Row 2 return: Draw B through first lp on hook, *ch 1, yo, draw through 2 lps on hook, rep from * across until 3 lps rem, ch 1, [yo, draw through 2 lps on hook] twice.

Row 3: *Tss, pick up lp in next ch-1 sp, rep from * across until 1 st rem, tss under both strands of last st. *(number of sts on hook is original number)*

Row 3 return: With A, yo, draw through 1 lp on hook, *yo, draw through 2 lps on hook, rep from * across until 1 lp rem on hook.

Rep rows 2 and 3 for desired length, ending with row 2 forward pass, work return with A. With A, bind off in sc following pattern for row 3. ■

Flecks & Pebbles

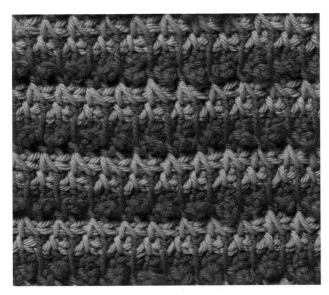

Multiple of any even number

PATTERN NOTE
Keep chain-5 pebbles to front of work.

SPECIAL STITCHES
Tunisian simple stitch decrease (tss dec): Tss *(see page 8)* under next 2 vertical bars as 1.

Slip 1 without working (sl 1 wow): Insert hook under next vertical bar, keeping this strand on hook, continue. *(This is an easy way to have 2 colors appear in a row while working with 1 color at a time.)*

INSTRUCTIONS
Row 1: With A, ch desired number, working in **back bump** *(see illustration)* of chs, pick up a lp in 2nd ch from hook and in each rem ch across, leaving all lps on hook.

Back Bar of Chain

Row 1 return: Yo, draw through 1 lp on hook, *yo, draw through 2 lps on hook, rep from * until 1 lp rem on hook.

Row 2: *Tss dec *(see Special Stitches)*, ch 5, pick up lp in 5th ch from hook, rep from * across until 1 st rem, tss under both strands of last st.

Row 2 return: Yo, draw through 1 lp on hook, *yo, draw through 2 lps on hook, rep from * across until 2 lps rem, with B, yo, draw through last 2 lps.

Row 3: *Ttws *(see page 12)*, sl 1 wow *(see Special Stitches)*, rep from * across until 1 st rem, tss under both strands of last st.

Row 3 return: Rep row 1 return.

Row 4: *Tss, ttws, rep from * across until 1 st rem, tss under both strands of last st.

Row 4 return: Rep row 2 return, changing to A.

Row 5: Tss, *tss dec, ch 5, pick up lp in 5th ch from hook, rep from * across until 2 sts rem, tss, tss under both strands of last st.

Row 5 return: Rep row 2 return.

Row 6: Tss, *ttws, sl 1 wow, rep from * across until 2 sts rem, tss, tss under both strands of last st.

Row 6 return: Rep row 1 return.

Row 7: 2 tss, *ttws, tss, rep from * across until 1 st rem, tss under both strands of last st.

Row 7 return: Rep row 4 return.

Rep rows 2–7 for desired length, ending after row 2 or 5 return, but do not change color.

Bind-off row: With A, *ttws, drawing through lp already on hook, rep from * across until 1 st rem, tss under both strands of last st, drawing through lp already on hook. ■

Net Overlay

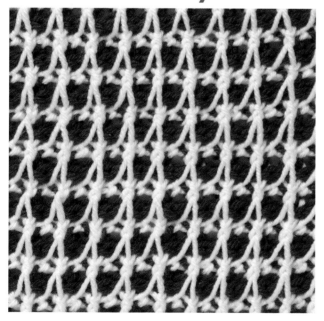

Multiple of any even number

SPECIAL STITCH

Tunisian simple stitch decrease (tss dec): Tss (*see page 8*) under next 2 vertical bars as 1.

INSTRUCTIONS

Row 1: Ch desired number, working in **back bump** (*see illustration*) of chs, pick up a lp in 2nd ch from hook and in each rem ch across, leaving all lps on hook.

Back Bar of Chain

Row 1 return: Yo, draw through 1 lp on hook, *yo, draw through 2 lps on hook, rep from * until 1 lp rem on hook.

Row 2: Tss in each st across until 1 st rem, tss under both strands of last st.

Row 2 return: Draw B through first lp on hook, *yo, draw through 2 lps on hook, rep from * across until 1 lp rem on hook.

Row 3: *Working 2 rows below, **tss dec** (*see Special Stitch*), ch 1, sk next st on current row, pick up lp under horizontal strand above next st on current row, rep from * across until 1 st rem, tss under both strands of last st.

Row 3 return: With A, yo, draw through 1 lp on hook, *yo, draw through 2 lps on hook, rep from * across until 1 lp rem on hook.

Rep rows 2 and 3 for desired length, ending with row 2 forward pass, work return with A. With A, bind off by *working 2 rows below, tss dec, ch 1 and draw through lp on hook, sk next st on current row, sl st under horizontal strand above next st on current row, rep from * across until 1 st rem, sl st under both strands of last st as if to tss. ■

Keyhole Scarf

SKILL LEVEL

INTERMEDIATE

FINISHED SIZE
One size fits most

FINISHED MEASUREMENTS
4¾ inches wide at widest point x 36 inches long

MATERIALS
- Deborah Norville Everyday Soft medium (worsted) weight acrylic yarn (4 oz/203 yds/113g per skein): 1 skein #1022 bittersweet
- Size L/11/8mm afghan crochet hook or size needed to obtain gauge
- Tapestry needle
- 2 locking stitch markers

GAUGE
With afghan hook: 14 tss = 4 inches; 12 rows = 4 inches

PATTERN NOTES
Tunisian crochet rows consist of 2 passes per row: a pick-up row and a work off or return pass. The right side of work is always facing.

In this pattern the return is not worked in standard way. Be sure to follow instructions carefully.

First vertical bar of row is skipped as that stitch is already on hook. This stitch is not referenced in instructions.

SPECIAL STITCHES
Tunisian purl stitch (tps): With yarn to front, insert hook under next vertical bar, bring yarn across front of vertical bar and to back, yo and draw through, keeping lp on hook.

Tunisian simple stitch (tss): Insert hook from right to left under next vertical bar or both lps of last st, yo and draw through, keeping lp on hook.

Tunisian chain loop (tchlp): Ch 7, remove lp from hook, insert hook through front bar of last Tunisian st worked, place lp back on hook and draw through, forming ch 7 into a lp.

Tunisian simple stitch decrease (tss dec): Insert hook under next 2 vertical bars, yo and draw through both bars.

SCARF
Note: *Before beginning work, wind approximately 10 yds of yarn into a small ball.*

BODY
Row 1 (RS): Ch 19, working in **back bar of ch** *(see illustration)*, pick up lp in 2nd ch from hook and in each rem ch across *(19 lps on hook)*, return: *yo, draw through 2 lps on hook, rep from * across until 1 lp rem.

Back Bar of Chain

Row 2: **Tps** *(see Special Stitches)* in each st across to last st, **tss** *(see Special Stitches)* under both lps of last st *(19 lps on hook)*, return: *yo, draw through 2 lps on hook, rep from * across until 1 lp rem.

Row 3: Tps in each of next 7 sts, **tchlp** *(see Special Stitches)*, tps in each of next 4 sts, tchlp, tps in each of next 6 sts, tss under both lps of last st *(19 lps on hook, 2 tchlps)*, return: keeping ch lps to front of work, *yo, draw through 2 lps on hook, rep from * across until 1 lp rem on hook.

Row 4: 2 tps, 13 tss, 2 tps, tss under both lps of last st (*19 lps on hook*), return: keeping ch lps to front of work, *yo, draw through 2 lps on hook, rep from * across until 1 lp rem on hook.

Row 5: 2 tps, 5 tss, tchlp; 4 tss, tchlp, 4 tss, 2 tps, tss under both lps of last st (*19 lps on hook, 2 tchlps*), return: keeping ch lps to front of work, *yo, draw through 2 lps on hook, rep from * across until 1 lp rem on hook.

Row 6: Rep row 4.

Row 7: 2 tps, 6 tss, tchlp, 2 tss, tchlp, 5 tss, 2 tps 2, tss under both lps of last st (*19 lps on hook, 2 tchlps*), return: keeping ch lps to front of work, *yo, draw through 2 lps on hook, rep from * across until 1 lp rem on hook.

Row 8: Rep row 4.

Row 9: 2 tps, 7 tss, tchlp, 6 tss, 2 tps, tss under both lps of last st (*19 lps on hook, 1 tchlp*), return: keeping ch lp to front of work, *yo, draw through 2 lps on hook, rep from * across until 1 lp rem.

Row 10: Rep row 4.

Row 11: Rep row 7.

Rows 12 & 13: Rep rows 4 and 5.

Row 14: Rep row 4.

Rows 15–24: Rep rows 5–14.

FIRST HALF OF KEYHOLE
Row 25: 2 tps, 5 tss, tchlp, tss, leave rem sts unworked (*9 lps on hook, 1 tchlp*), return: yo, draw through 1 lp on hook, keeping ch lp in front of work, *yo, draw through 2 lps on hook, rep from * across until 1 lp rem on hook.

Row 26: 2 tps, 3 tss, **tss dec** (*see Special Stitches*), tss under both lps of last st (*8 lps on hook*), return: yo, draw through 1 lp on hook, *yo, draw through 2 lps on hook, rep from * across until 1 lp rem on hook.

Row 27: 2 tps, 4 tss, tchlp, tss under both lps of last st (*8 lps on hook, 1 tchlp*), return: yo, draw

through 1 lp on hook, keeping ch lp in front of work, *yo, draw through 2 lps on hook, rep from * across until 1 lp rem on hook.

Row 28: 2 tps, 2 tss, tss dec, tss under both lps of last st (*7 lps on hook*), return: yo, draw through 1 lp on hook, *yo, draw through 2 lps on hook, rep from * across until 1 lp rem on hook.

Row 29: 2 tps, 3 tss, tchlp, tss under both lps of last st (*7 lps on hook, 1 tchlp*), return: yo, draw through 1 lp on hook, keeping ch lp in front of work, *yo, draw through 2 lps on hook, rep from * across until 1 lp rem on hook.

Row 30: 2 tps, 3 tss, tss under both lps of last st (*7 lps on hook*), return: yo, draw through 1 lp on hook, *yo, draw through 2 lps on hook, rep from * across until 1 lp rem on hook. Place lp on locking st marker.

2ND HALF OF KEYHOLE
Row 25: Sk first unworked st on row 24 from First Half of Keyhole, with yarn from small ball in next st, tss, tchlp, 5 tss, 2 tps, tss under both lps of last st (*9 lps on hook, 1 tchlp*), return: *yo, draw through 2 lps on hook, rep from * across until 1 lp rem on hook.

Row 26: Tss dec, 3 tss, 2 tps, tss under both lps of last st (*8 lps on hook*), return: *yo, draw through 2 lps on hook, rep from * across until 1 lp rem on hook

Row 27: Tchlp, 4 tss, 2 tps, tss through both lps of last st (*8 lps on hook, 1 tchlp*), return: keeping ch lp in front of work, *yo, draw through 2 lps on hook, rep from * across until 1 lp rem on hook.

Row 28: Tss dec, 2 tss, 2 tps, tss under both lps of last st (*7 lps on hook*), return: *yo, draw through 2 lps on hook, rep from * across until 1 lp rem on hook.

Row 29: Tchlp, 3 tss, 2 tps, tss under both lps of last st (*7 lps on hook, 1 tchlp*), return: keeping ch lp in front of work, *yo, draw through 2 lps on hook, rep from * across until 1 lp rem on hook.

Row 30: 3 tss, 2 tps, tss through both lps of last st (*7 lps on hook*), return: *yo, draw through

2 lps on hook, rep from * across until 1 lp rem on hook. Place lp on locking st marker. Fasten off.

REM OF BODY

Row 31: Place first marked lp back on hook, 2 tps, 3 tss, tchlp, tss, place 2nd marked lp back on hook, tss, tchlp, 3 tss, 2 tps, tss under both lps of last st (*15 lps on hook, 2 tchlps*), return: keeping ch lps in front of work, *yo, draw through 2 lps on hook, rep from * across until 1 lp rem on hook.

Row 32: 2 tps, 9 tss, 2 tps, tss under both lps of last st (*15 lps on hook*), return: *yo, draw through 2 lps on hook, rep from * across until 1 lp rem on hook.

Row 33: 2 tps, 5 tss, tchlp, 4 tss, 2 tps, tss under both lps of last st (*15 lps on hook, 1 tchlp*), return: keeping ch lp to front of work, *yo, draw through 2 lps on hook, rep from * across until 1 lp rem on hook.

Row 34: Rep row 32.

Row 35: 2 tps, 4 tss, tchlp, 2 tss, tchlp, 3 tss, 2 tps, tss under both lps of last st (*15 lps on hook, 2 tchlps*), return: keeping ch lps to front of work, *yo, draw through 2 lps on hook, rep from * across until 1 lp rem on hook.

Row 36: Rep row 32.

Row 37: 2 tps, 3 tss, tchlp, 4 tss, tchlp, 2 tss, 2 tps, tss under both lps of last st (*15 lps on hook, 2 tchlps*), return: keeping ch lps to front of work, *yo, draw through 2 lps on hook, rep from * across until 1 lp rem.

Row 38: Rep row 32.

Row 39: Rep row 37.

Row 40: Rep row 32.

Row 41: Rep row 35.

Row 42: Rep row 32.

Row 43: Rep row 33.

Rows 44–83: [Rep rows 34–43 consecutively] 4 times.

Rows 84–87: Rep rows 34–37.

Row 88: 2 tps, 2 tss, pick up lp under top strand of next horizontal st, 5 tss, pick up lp under top strand of next horizontal st, 2 tss, 2 tps, tss under both lps of last st (*17 lps on hook*), return: *yo, draw through 2 lps on hook, rep from * across until 1 lp rem on hook.

Row 89: 2 tps, 3 tss, tchlp, 5 tss, tchlp, 3 tss, 2 tps, tss under both lps of last st (*17 lps on hook, 2 tchlps*), return: keeping ch lps to front of work, *yo, draw through 2 lps on hook, rep from * across until 1 lp rem on hook.

Row 90: 2 tps, 3 tss, pick up lp under top strand of next horizontal st, 5 tss, pick up lp under top strand of next horizontal st, 3 tss, 2 tps, tss through both lps of last st (*19 lps on hook*), return: *yo, draw through 2 lps on hook, rep from * across until 1 lp rem on hook.

Rows 91–110: [Rep rows 5–14 consecutively] twice.

Rows 111 & 112: Rep rows 5 and 6.

Beg at row 3 and using photo as a guide, interlace ch lps, drawing each successive lp through lp below, at point where there is just 1 lp, pull lp through both of previous ch lps at same time, then pull both lps above through same lp and continue as before. After lacing, place ch lps in locking st markers.

Row 113: 6 tps, insert hook through next ch lp, remove marker, tps, securing ch lp in place, 3 tps, insert hook through next ch lp, remove marker, tps, securing ch lp in place, 6 tps, tss through both lps of last st (*19 lps on hook*), return: *yo, draw through 2 lps on hook, rep from * across until 1 lp rem on hook.

Row 114: Rep row 2.

Row 115: Working sl sts as if to tps, sl st in each vertical bar across. Fasten off. ∎

Tunisian Roll Brim Hat

SKILL LEVEL
INTERMEDIATE

FINISHED SIZE
One size fits most

FINISHED MEASUREMENT
24 inches in circumference

MATERIALS
- Deborah Norville Everyday Soft medium (worsted) weight acrylic yarn (4 oz/203 yds/113g per skein): 1 skein each #1022 bittersweet and #1021 magenta
- Size K/10½/6.5mm 22-inch cabled afghan crochet hook or size needed to obtain gauge
- Tapestry needle

Note: *Cabled afghan hook is required for ease of working body of Hat as sts wrap around top.*

GAUGE
With afghan hook: 16 tss = 4 inches; 12 rows = 4 inches

PATTERN NOTES
Tunisian crochet rows consist of 2 passes per row: a pick-up row and a work off or return pass. The right side of work is always facing.

First vertical bar of row is skipped as that stitch is already on hook. This stitch is not referenced in instructions.

Top of Hat is worked first in short row wedges to create a circle. Stitches are then picked up around circle and body of Hat is worked in rows, with a seam at center back.

Brim will naturally roll due to properties of tss.

To change color, yo and draw through last 2 lps with new color, dropping unused color to wrong side and fasten off.

SPECIAL STITCH
Tunisian simple stitch (tss): Insert hook from right to left under next vertical bar, yo and draw through keeping lp on hook.

HAT
TOP
FIRST WEDGE
Row 1 (RS): With bittersweet and leaving an 8-inch tail, ch 16, working in **back bar of ch** *(see illustration)*, pick up lp in 2nd ch from hook, leave rem chs unworked *(2 lps on hook)*,

return: yo, draw through 1 lp on hook, yo, draw through 2 lps on hook.

Back Bar of Chain

Row 2: Tss *(see Special Stitch)* in next st, working in back bump, pick up lp in next ch. *(3 lps on hook)*, return: yo, draw through 1 lp on hook,* yo, draw through 2 lps on hook, rep from * across until 1 lp rem on hook.

Rows 3–15: Tss in each st across, working in back bump, pick up lp in next ch *(16 lps on hook at end of row 15)*, return: yo, draw through 1 lp on hook, *yo, draw through 2 lps on hook, rep from * across until 1 lp rem on hook.

2ND WEDGE

Row 1: Tss in next st of last row of previous wedge, leave rem sts unworked *(2 lps on hook)*, return: yo, draw through 1 lp on hook, yo, draw through 2 lps on hook.

Rows 2–15: Rep rows 2–15 of First Wedge, working tss in next st of last row of previous wedge instead of foundation ch.

3RD–5TH WEDGES

Work same as 2nd Wedge.

6TH WEDGE

Rows 1–15: Rep rows 1–15 of 2nd Wedge.

Bind-off row: Sl st in each vertical bar across. Fasten off, leaving a long tail for sewing.

ASSEMBLY

With tapestry needle and long tail, **whipstitch** *(see illustration)* last Wedge to First Wedge. With beg tail, gather small opening at center and secure end.

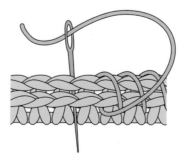

Whipstitch Edges

BODY

Row 1: With RS facing and beg at Top seam with bittersweet, [pick up 1 st under front lp of each of next 15 sts, yo] 5 times, pick up 1 st under front lp of each of next 15 sts, pick up 1 st in same place as first st of rnd *(96 lps on hook)*, return: yo, draw through 1 lp on hook, *yo, draw through 2 lps on hook, rep from * across until 1 lp rem on hook.

Row 2: Tss in each of next 7 sts, *yo, tss in each of next 16 sts, rep from * across to last 8 sts, yo, tss in each st, working last tss under both strands of last st *(102 lps on hook)*, return: yo, draw through 1 lp on hook, *yo, draw through 2 lps on hook, rep from * across until 1 lp rem on hook.

Row 3: Tss in each st, working last tss under both strands of last st *(102 lps on hook)*, return: yo, draw through 1 lp on hook, *yo, draw through 2 lps on hook, rep from * across until 1 lp rem on hook.

Rows 4–9: Rep row 3. At end of row 9, **change color** *(see Pattern Notes)* to magenta when working off last 2 lps.

Rows 10–12: Rep row 3, changing to A when working off last 2 lps of row 12.

Row 13: Rep row 3.

Row 14: Tss in each of next 8 sts, *yo, tss in each of next 17 sts, rep from * across to last 8 sts, yo, tss in each rem st, working last tss under both strands of last st *(108 lps on hook)*, return: yo, draw through 1 lp on hook, *yo, draw through 2 lps on hook, rep from * across until 1 lp rem on hook.

Row 15: Rep row 3.

Row 16: Tss in each of next 4 sts, *yo, tss in each of next 9 lps, rep from * across to last 4 sts, yo, tss in each rem st, working last tss under both strands of last st *(120 lps on hook)*, return: yo, draw through 1 lp on hook, *yo, draw through 2 lps on hook, rep from * across until 1 lp rem.

Row 17: Rep row 3.

Row 18: Tss in each of next 9 sts, *yo, tss in each of next 20 sts, rep from * across to last 10 sts, yo, tss in each rem st, working last tss under both strands of final st *(126 lps on hook)*, return: yo, draw through 1 lp on hook, *yo, draw through 2 lps on hook, rep from * across until 1 lp rem on hook.

Row 19: Rep row 3.

Row 20: Tss in each of next 5 sts, *yo, tss in each of next 10 sts, yo, tss in each of next 11 sts, rep from * across to last 5 sts, yo, tss in each rem st, working last tss under both strands of last st *(138 lps on hook)*, return: yo, draw through 1 lp on hook, *yo, draw through 2 lps on hook, rep from * across until 1 lp rem on hook.

Row 21: Rep row 3.

Row 22: Sl st in each vertical bar across. Fasten off, leaving a long tail for sewing.

FINISHING

With tapestry needle, sew center back seam using **Invisible Seam** *(see illustration)*. Block over wig form or bowl of appropriate size if desired. ■

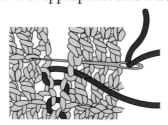

Invisible Seam

Tunisian Reader's Wrap

SKILL LEVEL

EASY

FINISHED SIZES

Instructions written for small/medium; changes for large/X-large are in [ ].

FINISHED MEASUREMENTS

19 [24] inches wide x 62 [68] inches long

MATERIALS

- Deborah Norville Everyday Soft medium (worsted) weight acrylic yarn (4 oz/203 yds/113g per skein):
  7 [8] skeins #1039 bright violet
- Size M/13/9mm 14-inch afghan crochet hook or size needed to obtain gauge
- Tapestry needle
- Sewing needle
- La petite #1056 hook closure by Blumenthal Lansing (optional)
- Matching sewing thread

GAUGE

With afghan hook in stitch pattern as for pocket:
29 sts = 8 inches; 12 rows = 4 inches

PATTERN NOTES

To adjust overall width, maintain same width for neck edge border and adjust width of main pattern by either adding or deleting chains in groups of 5. Each group of 5 chains will adjust width by about 1 inch. To adjust length, simply work more or fewer rows before working last 5 rows of Tunisian purl stitch. If size is adjusted, remember that more or less yarn than listed may be needed.

Tunisian crochet rows consist of 2 passes per row: a pick-up row and a work off or return pass. The right side of work is always facing.

In this pattern, the return is not worked in standard way. Be sure to follow instructions carefully.

First vertical bar of row is skipped as stitch is already on hook. This stitch is not referenced in instructions.

SPECIAL STITCHES

Tunisian simple stitch (tss): Insert hook from right to left under next vertical bar, yo and draw through, keeping lp on hook.

Tunisian purl stitch (tps): With yarn to front, insert hook under next vertical bar, bring yarn across front of vertical bar and to back, yo and draw through, keeping lp on hook.

Tunisian knit stitch (tks): Insert hook from front to back between strands of next vertical bar, yo and draw through, keeping lp on hook.

WRAP

Row 1 (RS): Ch 76 [91], working in **back bar of ch** *(see illustration)*, pick up lp in 2nd ch from hook and in each rem ch across *(76 [91] lps on hook)*, return: *yo, draw through 2 lps on hook, rep from * across until 1 lp rem on hook.

Back Bar of Chain

Row 2: [**Tss** *(see Special Stitches)*, **tps** *(see Special Stitches)*] 5 times, 2 tss, *tps, rep from * across to last st, tss under both strands of last st *(76 [91] lps on hook)*, return: *yo, draw through 2 lps on hook, rep from * across until 1 lp rem on hook.

Row 3: [Tps, tss] 5 times, tps, tss, *tps, rep from * across to last st, tss under both strands of last st *(76 [91] lps on hook)*, return: *yo, draw through 2 lps on hook, rep from * across until 1 lp rem on hook.

Rows 4 & 5: Rep rows 2 and 3.

Row 6: [Tss, tps] 5 times, tss, *tss, tps, tss, 2 **tks** *(see Special Stitches)*, rep from * across to last 4 sts, tss, tps, tss, tss under both strands of last st *(76 [91] lps on hook)*, return: yo, draw through 1 lp on hook, *yo, draw through 2 lps on hook, rep from * across until 1 lp rem on hook.

Row 7: [Tps, tss] 5 times, tps, *tss, tps, tss, 2 tks, rep from * across to last 4 sts, tss, tps, tss, tss under both strands of last st *(76 [91] lps on hook)*, return: yo, draw through 1 lp on hook, *yo, draw through 2 lps on hook, rep from * across until 1 lp rem on hook.

Rows 8–197 [8–213]: [Rep rows 6 and 7 alternately] 95 [103] times.

Rows 198 [214]: Rep row 6.

Rows 199–202 [215–218]: [Rep rows 2 and 3 alternately] twice.

Bind off in sl st in pattern.

POCKET
Make 2.

Row 1: Ch 31, working in back bump, pick up a lp in 2nd ch from hook and each rem ch across *(31 lps on hook)*, return: *yo, draw through 2 lps, rep from * across until 1 lp rem on hook.

Row 2: *Tss, tps, rep from * across to last 2 sts, tss, tss under both strands of last st *(31 lps on hook)*, return: *yo, draw through 2 lps, rep from * across until 1 lp rem on hook.

Row 3: *Tps, tss, rep from * across to last 2 sts, tps, tss under both strands of last st *(31 lps on hook)*, return: *yo, draw through 2 lps, rep from * across until 1 lp rem.

Rows 4–25: [Rep rows 2 and 3 alternately] 11 times.

Rows 26–29: Tps across to last st, tss under both strands of last st *(31 lps on hook)*, return: *yo, draw through 2 lps, rep from * across until 1 lp rem on hook.

Row 30: Working sl sts as if to tps, sl st in each vertical bar across. Fasten off, leaving long tail for sewing.

FINISHING
Block Wrap and Pockets.

Hold 1 Pocket with bound off edge at top and WS facing RS of Wrap, center Pocket directly above row 5 of Wrap or as desired. With tapestry needle and long tail, sew sides and bottom edge of Pocket to Wrap. Repeat with 2nd Pocket on opposite end.

If desired, using sewing thread, sew closure to front of Wrap approximately 21 inches above lower edge. ■

Tunisian Moebius Shawl

SKILL LEVEL

INTERMEDIATE

FINISHED SIZES

Instructions given fit size small; changes for medium, large and X-large are in [ ].

FINISHED MEASUREMENTS

18½ [19¾, 21, 23½] inches deep x 48 [50, 52, 54] inches in circumference

MATERIALS

- Deborah Norville Everyday Soft medium (worsted) weight acrylic yarn (4 oz/203 yds/113g per skein): 3 [3, 3, 4] skeins #1043 wild blue

4 MEDIUM

- Size L/11/8mm 22–40-inch cabled afghan crochet hook or size needed to obtain gauge
- Size K/10½/6.5mm crochet hook
- Tapestry needle

Note: *Cabled afghan hook is required for large number of stitches.*

GAUGE

With afghan hook in ext tss pattern: 13 sts = 4 inches; 6 rows = 4 inches

PATTERN NOTES

Tunisian crochet rows consist of 2 passes per row: a pick-up row and a work off or return pass. The right side of work is always facing.

Stitch created by a yarn over will look diagonal rather than vertical on following row.

SPECIAL STITCH

Extended Tunisian simple stitch (ext tss): Insert hook from right to left under next vertical bar, yo and draw through, ch 1, keeping lp on hook.

MOEBIUS

Rnd 1 (RS): Leaving 8-inch tail, ch 150 [156, 162, 168], working in **back bar of ch** (*see illustration*), pick up lp in 2nd ch from hook and in each rem ch across (*150 [156, 162, 168] lps on hook*), return: yo, draw through 1 lp on hook, *yo, draw through 2 lps on hook, rep from * across until 1 lp rem on hook, ch 1, to join rnd, carefully remove lp from hook, fold row in half with WS touching, place a full twist in row, insert hook under both strands of st to right (first lp worked off hook), place removed lp back on hook, yo, draw through lp and both strands of st just placed on hook. (*1 lp on hook*)

Note: *Use beginning tail and tapestry needle to close small gap at base of row.*

Back Bar of Chain

Rnd 2: *Yo, sk next st, **ext tss** (*see Special Stitches*), rep from * across to last st, yo, sk last st, insert hook in base of st to left (*first st of rnd*), yo and pull up a lp, yo and draw through 2 lps on hook (*150 [156, 162, 168] lps on hook*), return: yo, draw through 1 lp on hook, *yo, draw through 2 lps on hook, rep from * across until 1 lp rem on hook, ch 1; to join, carefully remove lp from hook, insert hook under both strands of st to right (first lp worked off hook), place removed lp back on hook, yo, draw through lp and both strands of st just placed on hook. (*1 lp on hook*)

Rnds 3–28 [3–30, 3–32, 3–36]: Rep rnd 2.

Rnd 29 [31, 33, 37]: Sl st in each vertical bar across.

Note: Place last lp on hook on regular crochet hook.

TOP EDGING

Rnd 1: Sc in each st around. Do not join.

Rnd 2: *Sc in each of next 3 sc, ch 2, sl st in last sc made, rep from * around, join with sl st in beg sc. Fasten off.

BOTTOM EDGING

Rnd 1: With RS facing and working in unused lps on opposite side of foundation ch, join yarn in same st where foundation ch was joined, sc in each ch around. Do not join.

Rnd 2: Rep rnd 2 of Top Edging.

FINISHING

There will be a diagonal line where rnds were joined. Move moebius twist around until diagonal line is concealed within twist. ■

Metric Conversion Charts

METRIC CONVERSIONS

yards	x	.9144	=	metres (m)
yards	x	91.44	=	centimetres (cm)
inches	x	2.54	=	centimetres (cm)
inches	x	25.40	=	millimetres (mm)
inches	x	.0254	=	metres (m)

centimetres	x	.3937	=	inches
metres	x	1.0936	=	yards

INCHES INTO MILLIMETRES & CENTIMETRES (Rounded off slightly)

inches	mm	cm	inches	cm	inches	cm	inches	cm
1/8	3	0.3	5	12.5	21	53.5	38	96.5
1/4	6	0.6	5 1/2	14	22	56	39	99
3/8	10	1	6	15	23	58.5	40	101.5
1/2	13	1.3	7	18	24	61	41	104
5/8	15	1.5	8	20.5	25	63.5	42	106.5
3/4	20	2	9	23	26	66	43	109
7/8	22	2.2	10	25.5	27	68.5	44	112
1	25	2.5	11	28	28	71	45	114.5
1 1/4	32	3.2	12	30.5	29	73.5	46	117
1 1/2	38	3.8	13	33	30	76	47	119.5
1 3/4	45	4.5	14	35.5	31	79	48	122
2	50	5	15	38	32	81.5	49	124.5
2 1/2	65	6.5	16	40.5	33	84	50	127
3	75	7.5	17	43	34	86.5		
3 1/2	90	9	18	46	35	89		
4	100	10	19	48.5	36	91.5		
4 1/2	115	11.5	20	51	37	94		

KNITTING NEEDLES CONVERSION CHART

Canada/U.S.	0	1	2	3	4	5	6	7	8	9	10	10½	11	13	15
Metric (mm)	2	2¼	2¾	3¼	3½	3¾	4	4½	5	5½	6	6½	8	9	10

CROCHET HOOKS CONVERSION CHART

Canada/U.S.	1/B	2/C	3/D	4/E	5/F	6/G	8/H	9/I	10/J	10½/K	N
Metric (mm)	2.25	2.75	3.25	3.5	3.75	4.25	5	5.5	6	6.5	9.0

ISBN: 978-1-59635-931-4

STITCH GUIDE

Need help? ▶ **StitchGuide.com** • ILLUSTRATED GUIDES • HOW-TO VIDEOS

STITCH ABBREVIATIONS

beg	begin/begins/beginning
bpdc	back post double crochet
bpsc	back post single crochet
bptr	back post treble crochet
CC	contrasting color
ch(s)	chain(s)
ch-	refers to chain or space previously made (i.e., ch-1 space)
ch sp(s)	chain space(s)
cl(s)	cluster(s)
cm	centimeter(s)
dc	double crochet (singular/plural)
dc dec	double crochet 2 or more stitches together, as indicated
dec	decrease/decreases/decreasing
dtr	double treble crochet
ext	extended
fpdc	front post double crochet
fpsc	front post single crochet
fptr	front post treble crochet
g	gram(s)
hdc	half double crochet
hdc dec	half double crochet 2 or more stitches together, as indicated
inc	increase/increases/increasing
lp(s)	loop(s)
MC	main color
mm	millimeter(s)
oz	ounce(s)
pc	popcorn(s)
rem	remain/remains/remaining
rep(s)	repeat(s)
rnd(s)	round(s)
RS	right side
sc	single crochet (singular/plural)
sc dec	single crochet 2 or more stitches together, as indicated
sk	skip/skipped/skipping
sl st(s)	slip stitch(es)
sp(s)	space(s)/spaced
st(s)	stitch(es)
tog	together
tr	treble crochet
trtr	triple treble
WS	wrong side
yd(s)	yard(s)
yo	yarn over

YARN CONVERSION

OUNCES TO GRAMS		GRAMS TO OUNCES	
1	28.4	25	7/8
2	56.7	40	1 2/3
3	85.0	50	1 3/4
4	113.4	100	3 1/2

UNITED STATES		UNITED KINGDOM
sl st (slip stitch)	=	sc (single crochet)
sc (single crochet)	=	dc (double crochet)
hdc (half double crochet)	=	htr (half treble crochet)
dc (double crochet)	=	tr (treble crochet)
tr (treble crochet)	=	dtr (double treble crochet)
dtr (double treble crochet)	=	ttr (triple treble crochet)
skip	=	miss

Reverse single crochet (reverse sc): Ch 1, sk first st, working from left to right, insert hook in next st from front to back, draw up lp on hook, yo and draw through both lps on hook.

Chain (ch): Yo, pull through lp on hook.

Single crochet (sc): Insert hook in st, yo, pull through st, yo, pull through both lps on hook.

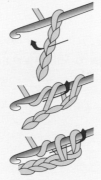

Double crochet (dc): Yo, insert hook in st, yo, pull through st, [yo, pull through 2 lps] twice.

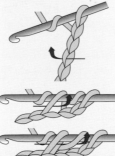

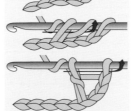

Front loop (front lp) Back loop (back lp)

Front Loop   Back Loop

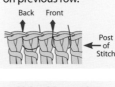

Front post stitch (fp): Back post stitch (bp): When working post st, insert hook from right to left around post of st on previous row.

Back   Front

Post of Stitch

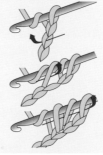

Half double crochet (hdc): Yo, insert hook in st, yo, pull through st, yo, pull through all 3 lps on hook.

Double treble crochet (dtr): Yo 3 times, insert hook in st, yo, pull through st, [yo, pull through 2 lps] 4 times.

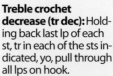

Slip stitch (sl st): Insert hook in st, pull through both lps on hook.

Chain color change (ch color change) Yo with new color, draw through last lp on hook.

Double crochet color change (dc color change) Drop first color, yo with new color, draw through last 2 lps of st.

Treble crochet (tr): Yo twice, insert hook in st, yo, pull through st, [yo, pull through 2 lps] 3 times.

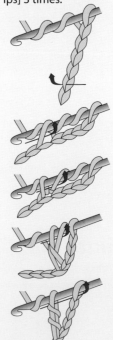

Single crochet decrease (sc dec): (Insert hook, yo, draw lp through) in each of the sts indicated, yo, draw through all lps on hook.

Example of 2-sc dec

Half double crochet decrease (hdc dec): (Yo, insert hook, yo, draw lp through) in each of the sts indicated, yo, draw through all lps on hook.

Example of 2-hdc dec

Double crochet decrease (dc dec): (Yo, insert hook, yo, draw lp through, yo, draw through 2 lps on hook) in each of the sts indicated, yo, draw through all lps on hook.

Example of 2-dc dec

Treble crochet decrease (tr dec): Holding back last lp of each st, tr in each of the sts indicated, yo, pull through all lps on hook.

Example of 2-tr dec